CW00507912

**Paper 1:** Epistemology and Moral Philosophy

# A-LEVEL
# PHILOSOPHY

revision exercises and exam practice workbook for
**AQA philosophy paper 1** (7172/1)

CHRISTIAN B. FEEST

First paperback edition July 2023

ISBN: 9798854042352

# Contents

## The Exam Format

The AQA philosophy A-level assessment is sat at the end of the course and consists of two 3-hour papers.

Paper 1 covers the epistemology and moral philosophy modules and has 100 available marks. Paper 2 covers the metaphysics of God and metaphysics of mind modules and also has 100 available marks. The format of each paper is always the same:

### Paper 1 (3 hrs)

| Epistemology | Moral philosophy |
|---|---|
| • 3 mark question<br>• 5 mark question<br>• 5 mark question<br>• 12 mark question<br>• 25 mark question | • 3 mark question<br>• 5 mark question<br>• 5 mark question<br>• 12 mark question<br>• 25 mark question |

**100 available marks, 50% of overall grade**

### Paper 2 (3 hrs)

| Metaphysics of God | Metaphysics of mind |
|---|---|
| • 3 mark question<br>• 5 mark question<br>• 5 mark question<br>• 12 mark question<br>• 25 mark question | • 3 mark question<br>• 5 mark question<br>• 5 mark question<br>• 12 mark question<br>• 25 mark question |

**100 available marks, 50% of overall grade**

## Assessment Objectives

The question formats are graded according to two "assessment objectives":

### AO1: 3, 5, and 12 mark questions

Assessment objective 1 (AO1) is **knowledge and understanding**.

The 3, 5, and 12 mark questions are 100% AO1. This means that you only have to explain the idea or argument you are asked about – you don't have to assess that idea or argument or say whether it is correct or not.

### AO2: 25 mark questions

Assessment objective 2 (AO2) is **analysis and evaluation**.

**It is only the 25 mark questions where AO2 comes in.** In the 25 mark questions, you will have to philosophically evaluate ideas and argue towards a conclusion. There is a specific formula for how to construct these answers that is described below.

# Question Types

## 3 marks

3 mark questions will ask you to define a simple philosophical concept, such as substance dualism or analytic truth. Don't write too much – just a sentence or two explaining the idea and an example (if applicable) is sufficient to get full marks. Including irrelevant information (e.g. evaluation) will actually lose you marks.

## 5 marks

5 mark questions are very similar to 3 mark questions except you will be asked to explain a slightly more detailed concept or argument. Again, don't write too much – just define any key terms in the question and then explain the idea or concept. Don't miss any details, but don't include irrelevant/redundant information (e.g. evaluation) either.

## 12 marks

12 mark questions are still 100% AO1. The topics you will be asked about will require you to write a bit more, but you still only have to explain an idea or argument – you don't have to evaluate whether it is correct or not.

These 12 mark questions are where you're most likely to slip into evaluation mode when you shouldn't. For example, say you get asked to explain how hallucinations and illusions are a problem for direct realism, just explain what direct realism is and how hallucinations and illusions are a problem for it – nothing more. You shouldn't give your opinion on whether direct realism is correct or not, or whether the hallucination argument is a successful objection or not. If you find yourself making arguments along these lines and giving your opinion on direct realism then you've gone too far! Often, students panic that they haven't written enough and so start adding in this kind of evaluation – don't do this! It's a waste of time and will lose you marks.

As always, a good place to start your answer is by defining the key terms in the question.

## 25 marks

Whereas the other questions only require you to *explain* an idea or argument, the 25 mark questions require evaluation: You have to argue for a particular philosophical viewpoint. In other words, you have to take a stance on a topic and argue that it is the correct one.

There is a pretty standard template for constructing these answers – and it's very important that your essay follows this template (at least roughly). If you don't include an introduction or a conclusion, for example, it's very difficult for an examiner to give more than around 10 marks out of 25.

The format of your 25 mark responses should look something like the template below:

- Introduction: Define key terms and then explain which side you are arguing for (E.g. "...In this essay I will argue for theory X")
- Argument for theory X
  - Possible response to this argument
    - Response to this response
- Argument against theory X
  - Response to this argument
- Conclusion: Theory X is correct because of the arguments above

You don't have to follow this template exactly, but there are several important features your essay will need to have if it is to achieve the top grade boundary: an introduction, a consistent argument, a balanced argument, and a conclusion.

## How to Use this Workbook

This workbook covers topics in paper 1 (epistemology and moral philosophy). It includes various exercises based around the four types of exam questions above. These exercises are designed to test your knowledge of the AQA philosophy course content and reinforce how to communicate that knowledge it in the exam to achieve maximum marks.

The question formats include multiple choice, fill-in-the-blanks, and some extended writing bits. There's not always a single correct answer – especially for the extend writing bits – but answers/suggestions to the epistemology questions can be found on page 39 and answers/suggestions to the moral philosophy questions can be found on page 79.

For questions covering paper 2 (metaphysics of God and mind), please see the *A-level Philosophy revision exercises and exam practice workbook for AQA philosophy paper 2 (7172/2)* available from philosophyalevel.com.

## Definitions of Knowledge

**Outline the tripartite definition of knowledge and explain how Gettier cases challenge this definition.** *(12 marks)*

The tripartite definition of knowledge defines knowledge as 1. _____

2. _____ 3. _____. According to this definition,

these 3 conditions are both necessary and _____ for

knowledge. However, Gettier cases challenge the tripartite definition of knowledge.

In the first Gettier case, Smith and Jones are interviewing for the same job. Smith

overhears the interviewer say _____

_____ .

Smith also sees Jones count 10 coins from his pocket. From this, Smith forms the

belief that _____

_____

However, after Smith and Jones finish the interview, Smith gets the job, not Jones.

And when Smith looks in his pocket, he sees that, by coincidence, he too has 10 coins

in his pocket. So, Smith's *belief* that _____

_____

was _____ and _____ ,

and therefore meets all 3 conditions of the tripartite definition of knowledge.

However, Smith's belief was not really knowledge, because it was just a lucky coincidence that he also had 10 coins in his pocket. This shows you can have a belief that meets all 3 conditions of the tripartite definition of knowledge, and yet is not knowledge. This shows that although the 3 conditions of the tripartite definition may be necessary for knowledge, they are not a _____ definition of knowledge.

## How does adding a 'no false lemmas' condition to the tripartite definition of knowledge avoid Gettier cases? *(5 marks)*

A false lemma is a false premise or assumption used to arrive at a conclusion. In the example of the first Gettier case, the false lemma is Smith's belief that _____

_____

when, in reality, *Smith* gets the job. From this *false* lemma (and from seeing Jones count 10 coins from his pocket), Smith infers the belief that "The man who gets the job has 10 coins in his pocket". Smith's belief here is true and _____ ,

so meets all 3 conditions of the tripartite definition of knowledge. However, it does not count as knowledge because _____

_____ . By adding a 'no false lemmas' condition to the tripartite definition, we can correctly say Smith's belief does not count as knowledge because it is derived from the false lemma that _____

_____ .

**➔ Match the definition of knowledge (left) to its description (right).**

1. Tripartite

2. Infallibilism

3. Reliabilism

4. Virtue epistemology

A. True belief formed via a reliable method

B. Apt belief (Sosa's AAA definition)

C. True belief justified so that it's certain/impossible to doubt

D. Justified true belief

---

**➔ Match the type of knowledge (left) to its description (right).**

1. Propositional

2. Ability

3. Acquaintance

A. Knowledge *how* (e.g. knowing how to ride a bike)

B. Knowledge *of* (e.g. "I know Christian well")

C. Knowledge *that* (e.g. "I know that 2+2=4")

---

**⑦ Multiple choice: Select the correct answer(s) from the boxes below.**

Which of the following are examples of **intellectual virtues**?

☐ Being biased.

☐ Being open-minded.

☐ Jumping to conclusions.

☐ Caring about the truth.

☐ Being closed-minded.

☐ Ignoring evidence.

☐ Caring about evidence.

☐ Being rational.

---

**⑦ Multiple choice: Select the correct answer(s) from the boxes below.**

**Fake Barn County** is an issue for which definition(s) of knowledge?

☐ Justified true belief.

☐ Reliabilism.

☐ No false lemmas.

☐ Infallibilism.

## What is reliabilism? *(3 marks)*

Reliabilism is a definition of knowledge which says *S* knows *P* if:

1. *P* is _____ .

2. *S* _____ that *P*.

3. *S*'s _____ that *P* is formed via a _____

method.

## What is ability knowledge? *(3 marks)*

Ability knowledge, sometimes referred to as "knowledge

how", is knowledge of things like skills, movements, and

how to perform actions. For example, _____

_____

_____ .

**Exam tip:**
*Examples* are an easy and effective way to demonstrate knowledge and understanding.

## What is virtue epistemology? *(3 marks)*

Virtue epistemology definitions of knowledge invoke _____ virtues,

such as being rational and _____. For example,

virtue epistemology may define knowledge by saying *S* knows that *P* if: 1. *P* is true, 2.

*S* believes that *P*, and 3. *S*'s belief that *P* is a result of *S* successfully using their

_____ virtues.

## What is infallibilism?    *(3 marks)*

Infallibilist definitions of knowledge require beliefs to be true and justified in such a way that they are _____ (i.e. impossible to doubt). For example, if a belief could be false due to sceptical scenarios such as _____ _____ then it would not count as knowledge according to infallibilism.

## How should propositional knowledge be defined?    *(25 marks)*

**Introduction:** In this essay we are defining *propositional* knowledge, not acquaintance or _____ knowledge. In this essay, I will consider various definitions of propositional knowledge but argue that none succeed in correctly providing the necessary and sufficient conditions.

**Exam tip:**
25 mark questions are the **only** questions that award marks for **evaluation** (AO2).

*Suggested paragraph starters:*

**Tripartite definition:**  The tripartite definition of defines knowledge as...

**Gettier cases:**  However, Gettier cases provide a counterexample to the tripartite definition and show that it is not....

**No false lemmas:**  A post-Gettier definition of knowledge aims to salvage the tripartite definition of knowledge against Gettier cases by adding...

**Fake Barn County:**  However, the Fake Barn County counterexample shows that...

**Double-luck counterexamples:**  Zagzebski argues that any definition of knowledge that *adds* 'truth' and 'justification' (such as those considered above) will fail because of Gettier-style cases. To create a Gettier style case for a definition of knowledge...

**Infallibilism:**  Infallibilist definitions claim that knowledge must be justified in such a way that it is certain or impossible to doubt. This avoids Gettier cases because...

**Too strict:**  However, the infallibilist definition of knowledge is too strict...

**Conclusion:**  In conclusion, ...

**Paragraph practice: The PEEL format**

**PEEL** stands for **Point**, **Evidence** (or Example), **Explanation**, **Link**. It's a good way to structure your paragraphs when writing – especially with the 25 mark essay questions – as it encourages you to go into detail and make clear what each argument shows.

Below is an example of how you could use this PEEL format to structure the paragraph in the essay above that responds to the infallibilist definition of knowledge:

**Point:** The infallibilist definition of knowledge is too strict.

**Evidence/Example:** Infallibilist definitions of knowledge say that knowledge is true belief that must be justified in such a way that it is certain and impossible to doubt. However, there are many instances of beliefs that qualify as 'knowledge' that are not certain. For example, my belief that "Paris is the capital of France" could be false – I may be being deceived by an evil demon, or have been lied to all my life, or I could be hallucinating, and so on – and so these possible reasons for doubt mean my belief does not count as knowledge according to infallibilism.

**Explanation:** However, these scenarios are not realistic reasons to doubt the belief that "Paris is the capital of France". Even though I can't be 100% certain of this belief, it is still clearly an example of knowledge, and yet infallibilism would say it is not an example of knowledge. This shows that the infallibilist definition of knowledge is too strict.

**Link:** The correct definition of 'knowledge' must provide necessary and sufficient conditions for the term. But this example shows that certainty/the impossibility of doubt is not necessary for knowledge, and thus the infallibilist definition of knowledge fails.

*Now you try!* The example paragraph below uses the **PEEL** format to make the Fake Barn County objection to the no false lemmas definition of knowledge.

**Point:** The Fake Barn County counter example shows that the no false lemmas definition of knowledge fails.

**Evidence/Example:** In this counter example, Henry is driving through Fake Barn County. In Fake Barn County _____

_____ .

Whenever Henry looks at one of the fake barns, he forms the belief "That's a barn", but his belief is false because _____ .

However, when Henry looks at the one real barn, he forms the same belief and this time it is 1. _____ 2. _____ and

3. _____ .

**Explanation:** Thus, Henry's belief when he looks at the one real barn meets all four conditions of the no false lemmas definition of knowledge. However, it is not really knowledge because _____

_____

_____

**Link:** The Fake Barn County example shows that the no false lemmas definition of knowledge is not a _____ definition of knowledge because it is possible for something to meet all the conditions of this definition and yet not be knowledge.

# Knowledge from Perception

## Outline the argument from illusion against direct realism. *(5 marks)*

Direct realism is the claim that what we perceive are

mind-_____ objects and their properties.

The argument from illusion challenges direct realism

because in cases of illusion what we are perceiving is

not a mind-_____ object or a property of

it. For example, a stick may look _____ to

us when in water but in reality it does not have the

property of being _____ . This shows that

our _____ of the stick is different to

the mind-_____ reality of the stick, and so what we are perceiving is

not a mind-_____ object or its properties, as direct realism claims.

**Exam tip:**

**As a 5 mark question, 100% of the marks here are for AO1**. Even though we are *describing* an argument against direct realism, we are not *evaluating* direct realism or whether the argument from illusion succeeds.

## Explain how Berkeley's idealism differs from indirect realism. *(5 marks)*

The main difference between idealism and indirect realism concerns the existence of

the mind-independent world: Indirect realism says _____

_____ (so is a *realist* theory) whereas idealism says

_____

(so is an *anti-realist* theory). Another difference is that idealism is a *direct* theory of

perception because it says _____

_____ , whereas indirect realism

says we perceive (mind-independent) reality *indirectly* via _____ .

**Outline the argument that indirect realism leads to scepticism about the existence of mind-independent objects and explain Russell's response that the external world is the best hypothesis.** *(12 marks)*

 Missing words: **justify, indirectly, abductive, mind-dependent, perceiving, hypothesis, mind-independent, sense data, scepticism**

Indirect realism is the claim that a _____ external world exists, but that we perceive it _____ via _____ . As this _____ is _____ according to indirect realism, we never perceive the _____ external world itself, which means we cannot _____ a belief in it. This leads to _____ about whether we can know _____ objects exist at all (this is sometimes called the veil of perception).

Russell's response to the veil of perception is to accept that we cannot deductively *prove* the existence of _____ objects, so we should instead treat _____ objects as a _____ . This is an example of an _____ argument. Russell uses the example of his cat to demonstrate why the _____ objects hypothesis is better than alternatives. Firstly, _____ objects *connect* our perceptions. For example, if the cat exists mind-independently, it explains why I see it in one location and then at another location later on: The cat moves from one location to the other when I wasn't looking. In contrast, if the cat does not exist mind-independently, then it does not exist when I am not _____ it and springs into existence in a new location next time I look, which seems an unlikely explanation. Secondly, the mind-independent objects hypothesis explains why the cat gets hungry between meals even when I am not _____ it: The cat exists mind-independently and gets progressively more hungry even when I'm not looking. However, if the cat does not exist independently of my mind, it wouldn't make sense why it would get more hungry when I'm not _____ it because it wouldn't exist during that time. These examples show the _____ objects hypothesis has better explanatory power than the hypothesis that everything is _____ and so _____

_____ .

## Outline Berkeley's 'master argument' for idealism.    *(5 marks)*

Berkley's idealism is the view that _____

_____ . To prove idealism, Berkeley's master argument attempts to demonstrate that mind-independent objects are impossible in the form of a dialogue. In the dialogue, Philonous asks Hylas to conceive of a tree that _____

_____ . Hylas responds by saying he is imagining a tree that is not being perceived by anyone. However, Philonous responds to Hylas that the tree he is imagining cannot be mind-_____ at all since it is being conceived of by Hylas himself! Berkeley takes this to show that mind-_____ objects are *inconceivable* and therefore *impossible*. If mind-_____ objects are impossible, then everything must be mind-_____ and thus idealism is correct.

## Multiple choice: Select the correct answer(s) from the boxes below.

According to **indirect realism**, what are the immediate objects of perception?

☐ Mind-independent objects.

☐ Mind-independent sense data.

☐ Mind-dependent sense data.

☐ Ideas.

## → Match the theory of perception (left) to its description (right).

1. Direct realism

A. A mind-independent world exists and we perceive it indirectly via mind-dependent sense data.

2. Indirect realism

B. The immediate objects of perception are mind-dependent ideas. Mind-independent objects do not exist.

3. Idealism

C. The immediate objects of perception are mind-independent objects and their properties.

## Multiple choice: Select the correct answer(s) from the boxes below.

Which of the following are **arguments against direct realism**?

☐ Veil of perception/scepticism.

☐ Perceptual variation.

☐ Time lag.

☐ Hallucination.

## Multiple choice: Select the correct answer(s) from the boxes below.

Which of the following are **arguments against Berkeley's idealism**?

☐ Illusion.

☐ Hallucination.

☐ The master argument.

☐ God doesn't change but perceptions do.

☐ Perceptual variation.

☐ Solipsism.

## Assess direct realism. *(25 marks)*

A good 25 mark response argues **consistently** for a particular philosophical position. In the case of this question, the two obvious positions are: 1. Direct realism is *true*, or 2. Direct realism is *false*. However, to get top marks, your essay can't be one-sided: You have to consider possible *objections* and *respond* to them. Use the spaces below to plan a consistent and balanced response to this 25 mark question on direct realism.

**Introduction:** In this essay I will argue that _____
_____ .

**Argument for my side:** _____
_____ .

**Response to this argument:** _____
_____ .

**Counter-response defending my side:** _____
_____ .

**Objection to my side:** _____
_____ .

**Response to this objection defending my side:** _____
_____ .

**Conclusion:** _____
_____
_____
_____ .

**Exam tip:**

**Don't introduce new ideas in your conclusion** – it should be a 'summing up' of arguments that follows logically from what you've written above.

Although not specifically mentioned on the syllabus, the **'relational properties'** argument defending direct realism is worth remembering as it can respond to illusion *and* perceptual variation. Below is how it may be broken down using the **PEEL** format.

**Point:** The concept of relational properties can defend the direct realist's claim that

what we perceive are mind-_____ objects and their properties.

**Evidence/Example:** Relational properties are mind-independent but which relational

property someone perceives will differ relative to their location. For example, England

has the (mind-independent) properties of being *south* of Iceland but being *north* of

France. So, in some sense, England has both the (mind-independent) property of being

north *and* the (mind-independent) property of being south simultaneously. However,

which one of these two properties (northness or southness) a person perceives will

vary depending on whether they are in Iceland or France.

**Explanation:** The same reasoning can be applied to cases of perceptual variation. For

example, _____

_____

_____

_____

_____ .

**Link:** This shows that perceptual variation does not disprove direct realism because

_____

_____

_____ .

## Is indirect realism a convincing theory of perception?   *(25 marks)*

*Possible paragraph starters:*

**Introduction:** Indirect realism is a theory of perception which says that a mind-independent external world exists and that... In this essay I will argue that...

**Avoids issues with direct realism:** An advantage of indirect realism is it is able to account for differences between perception and reality. For example, ...

**Veil of perception:** However, a distinction between sense data and mind-independent reality raises the issue of scepticism about the existence of the external world....

**Response 1:** In response, Locke argues the involuntary nature of perception shows...

**Counter-response:** However, dreaming is an example of involuntary perception and yet it is not caused by anything external. This weakens Locke's argument because...

**Response 2:** A more effective response is Russell's argument that the external world...

**Conclusion:** In conclusion, indirect realism is a convincing theory of perception...

## Assess Berkeley's idealism.   *(25 marks)*

*Possible paragraph starters:*

**Introduction:** Idealism is a theory of perception which says that the immediate objects of perception are mind-dependent ideas. In this essay, I will argue that...

**Berkeley's master argument:** A key argument in favour of idealism is...

**Response:** However, the master argument fails to prove idealism because it conflates *the idea of* a mind-independent object with a mind-independent object *itself*....

**Idealism leads to solipsism:** An issue for idealism is that it leads to solipsism. Solipsism is the view that...

**Response:** Berkeley's argument that God is the cause of perception provides a potential response to the solipsism objection...

**Counter-response:** However, there are several issues with the role of God in Berkeley's theory. For example, Berkeley says that God is unchanging and yet...

**Hallucination:** A further issue for idealism is cases of hallucination...

**Conclusion:** In conclusion, ...

# Knowledge from Reason

## What is an analytic truth?    (3 marks)

☑ Complete the answer by ticking the appropriate boxes below.

An analytic truth is something that is….

☐ true in virtue of how the external world is.

☐ true in virtue of the meaning of the words.

For example….

☐ "grass is green" is an analytic truth.

☐ "a bachelor is an unmarried man" is an analytic truth.

## What is *a posteriori* knowledge?    (3 marks)

☑ Complete the answer by ticking the appropriate boxes below.

A *posteriori* knowledge is….

☐ Knowledge that can be known prior to experience of the external world.

☐ Knowledge that requires experience of the external world before it can be known.

For example….

☐ Mathematical truths (e.g. "1+1=2") can be worked out purely using thinking/reason and so are a posteriori.

☐ "Paris is the capital of France" requires experience to verify (e.g. looking at a map) and so is a posteriori.

**Multiple choice: Select the correct answer(s) from the boxes below.**

Which of the following are **arguments <u>for</u> innate knowledge**?

☐ Locke's primary and secondary qualities.

☐ Meno's slave.

☐ Leibniz's argument from necessary truths.

☐ Locke's tabula rasa theory.

---

**Multiple choice: Select the correct answer(s) from the boxes below.**

Which of the following are **contingent truths**?

☐ 1+1=2.

☐ It's impossible for something to be true and false.

☐ Grass is green.

☐ Paris is the capital of France.

---

**Multiple choice: Select the correct answer(s) from the boxes below.**

Which of the following sources of knowledge are *a priori*?

☐ Rational intuition.

☐ A science experiment.

☐ Visual perception.

☐ Logical deduction.

---

**Multiple choice: Select the correct answer(s) from the boxes below.**

Which of the following does **rationalism** claim?

☐ All knowledge of synthetic truths comes from a posteriori observation.

☐ All knowledge of synthetic truths comes from a priori intuition and deduction.

☐ Some knowledge of synthetic truths can come from a priori intuition and deduction.

☐ There is no such thing as innate knowledge.

Innatism is the view that _____

_____ .

Through reason, we are able to realise this knowledge and hence innate knowledge is

*a priori*.

Leibniz argues that knowledge of necessary truths is innate. A necessary truth is

something that must be true in every possible world. For example, the law of non-

contradiction (e.g. "it is impossible for A to be true and not A to be true ") and

mathematical truths (e.g. "2+2=4") are examples of necessary truths. In contrast,

_____ truths are true but could have been false. For example,

_____

_____ .

Leibniz notes that experience can only tell us about truths in *specific instances*. For

example, if I take *these* 2 apples and add them to *these* other 2 apples, my experience

tells me that I have 4 apples *in this instance*. However, even without further

experience, I know that adding *any* 2 things to *any* 2 other things will always give 4

things – I can see "2+2=4" is true *necessarily*. I can see that "2+2=4" must be true in

every possible instance even *without experience* of every possible instance. Leibniz

takes this to demonstrate innate knowledge because _____

_____

## Explain the view that the mind is a 'tabula rasa' at birth.    *(5 marks)*

 ***You're the examiner!* Use the mark scheme below to mark the example answers.**

| 5/5 | A full, clear and precise explanation. The student makes logical links between precisely identified points, with no redundancy. |
|---|---|
| 4/5 | A clear explanation, with logical links, but some imprecision/redundancy. |
| 3/5 | The substantive content of the explanation is present and there is an attempt at logical linking, but the explanation is not full and/or precise. |
| 2/5 | One or two relevant points made, but not precisely. The logic is unclear. |
| 1/5 | Fragmented points, with no logical structure. |
| 0/5 | Nothing written worthy of credit. |

'Tabula rasa' is Latin for 'blank slate'. It is a view of the mind at birth held by empiricist philosophers, such as John Locke, who believe that there is no such thing as innate knowledge or innate concepts and so the mind at birth is completely empty. Since no concepts or knowledge exist prior to experience according to this view, all concepts and knowledge must come from experience. According to Locke's account of this, knowledge and concepts are gained through two forms of experience: Sensation and reflection. Through these two types of experience, we can go from a blank slate/tabula rasa to gaining and possessing knowledge and concepts.

                                                             _____ / 5

The tabula rasa theory says that knowledge comes from experience. It is the view held by Locke. Plato argues against this view with the slave boy. The slave boy knows the answers, which disproves the tabula rasa theory. However, Locke would respond that a baby doesn't know anything when it is born, which supports the tabula rasa theory.

_____ / 5

## Does innate knowledge exist?  *(25 marks)*

*Possible paragraph starters:*

**Introduction:** Empiricists, such as Locke, argue that the mind at birth is a tabula rasa. However, innatists argue that humans are born with innate (propositional) knowledge. In this essay, I will defend innatism and argue that innate knowledge does exist.

**Plato and the slave boy:** In the *Meno* dialogue, Plato attempts to demonstrate that a slave boy has innate knowledge of geometry...

**Response:** However, Plato's example is not the strongest example of innate knowledge as it's possible the slave is instead just using reason to work out the answer...

**Leibniz's argument from necessary truths:** A more effective argument for innate knowledge is Leibniz's argument that knowledge of necessary truths is innate...

**Exam tip:**
You don't have to accept *every* argument that supports your conclusion. The 21-25 grade boundary mentions *"crucial arguments are clearly identified against less crucial ones"*. Notice how this is done in this example.

**'Children and idiots' response (Locke):** Locke would respond that necessary truths are not innately known as they are not universally held. For example, ....

**Counter-response (Leibniz's marble analogy):** However, Leibniz never claimed that necessary truths are fully formed in the mind at birth. Instead, like a block of marble...

**Conclusion:** In conclusion, even though Plato's slave boy example does not conclusively prove the existence of innate knowledge, Leibniz's argument...

**Outline the meaning of 'intuition' and 'deduction' within Descartes' approach to gaining knowledge.** *(5 marks)*

Intuition and deduction are *a p_____* methods of gaining knowledge, meaning they do not require sensory experience of the external world. For Descartes, (rational) intuition is the ability of the mind to see "_____ and _____ ideas" are true (and impossible to be false) purely by thinking. An example of this is his _____ argument, "I exist", which is known purely by intuition. Deduction is the use of deductively v_____ reasoning to derive further conclusions that must necessarily follow from this foundational knowledge.

**Multiple choice: Select the correct answer(s) from the boxes below.**

In *Meditations*, which **3 synthetic truths** does Descartes attempt to prove by using *a priori* intuition and deduction?

☐ An evil demon exists.

☐ I exist.

☐ Grass is green.

☐ The external world exists.

☐ God exists.

☐ The external world does not exist.

**➡ Match the argument (left) to its conclusion (right).**

| | |
|---|---|
| 1. Evil demon | A. "God exists" |
| 2. Cogito argument | B. "I must doubt all claims of knowledge" |
| 3. Trademark argument | C. "The external world exists" |
| 4. Proof of the external world | D. "I exist" |

## Briefly explain Hume's fork. *(5 marks)*

According to Hume's fork, there are two (and only two) types of judgements of reason:

1. Relations of _____ , and 2. Matters of _____ .

The key feature of a relation of _____ is that it *cannot* be denied without

leading to a _____ . For example, "triangles have 3 sides" is a

relation of _____ because _____

_____ . Relations of

_____ can thus be known purely *a priori*.

The key feature of a matter of _____ is that it *can* be denied without

leading to a _____ . For example, even though "grass is green" is

true, it's logically possible _____

_____ . So, in order to know

a matter of _____ , we require empirical experience and thus matters of

_____ can only be known *a posteriori*.

## What is empiricism? *(3 marks)*

Empiricism is the view that all (or at least most) knowledge comes from

_____ and so all knowledge is *a p*_____ .

Empiricists reject the existence of innate propositional knowledge and reject the claim

of rationalist philosophers that *a priori* reasoning methods (such as _____

and deduction) alone can establish knowledge of _____ truths.

**To what extent can knowledge be acquired, *a priori*, using intuition and deduction? (25 marks)**

*Possible paragraph starters:*

**Introduction:** Rationalist philosophers, such as Descartes, believe that knowledge of some synthetic truths can be acquired purely *a priori*. Empiricist philosophers, such as Hume, deny this claim and argue that *a priori* methods can only demonstrate analytic truths and that all synthetic truths are known *a posteriori*. In this essay, I will defend rationalism by demonstrating that at least one synthetic truth can be known via *a priori* intuition and deduction.

**Descartes' trademark argument:** In *Meditations*, Descartes argues that "God exists" can be demonstrated purely via *a priori* intuition and deduction...

**Hume's fork response:** Hume's Fork states that there are two judgements of reason: Relations of ideas and matters of fact. A relation of ideas is.... whereas a matter of fact is.... Applying Hume's fork to the various premises of the trademark argument reveals it is not entirely *a priori*. For example, the premise that...

**Descartes' cogito argument:** A stronger argument for rationalism is Descartes' cogito argument...

**Hume's fork response:** However, Hume would argue that "I exist" does not follow *a priori* from "I think" because "everything that thinks exists" is not a relation of ideas. This is demonstrated by the fact that there is no logical contradiction in the idea of a thought without a thinker. For example, ....

**Exam tip:**
Answers in the top grade boundary will demonstrate **precise use of philosophical language**. Here, this means using terms like *'synthetic truth'*, *'empiricism'*, and *'a priori knowledge'* correctly as well as explaining how they relate to each other and the overall essay.

**Counter-response:** But even if "I exist" does not follow *a priori*, "thoughts exist" or "this thought exists" are still synthetic truths. So, it can be argued that...

**Conclusion:** In conclusion, although intuition and deduction cannot establish many synthetic truths a priori, there is at least one synthetic truth that can be known purely via intuition and deduction. Although the trademark argument and, to a lesser extent, the cogito argument fail to establish rationalism, this essay has demonstrated that...

**Briefly explain Descartes' trademark argument for the existence of God and explain how Hume's fork might be applied to this argument.** *(12 marks)*

The best answers will make **logical links** between precisely identified points crystal clear. In the response below, the use of numbered premises enable us to apply Hume's fork to a specific claim in Descartes' argument and explain what this shows.

Descartes' trademark argument is an attempt to use intuition and deduction to establish God's existence *a priori*. The key points are as follows:

1. I have the idea of God, which is the idea of an infinite and perfect being.

2. The cause of an effect must have as much reality as the effect.

3. Therefore the cause of my idea of God must have as much reality as an infinite and perfect being.

4. Therefore an infinite and perfect being (God) exists.

According to Hume's fork, there are only two judgements of reason: Relations of ideas and matters of fact. A relation of ideas can be known entirely *a priori*, since its negation leads to contradiction and is thus inconceivable in the mind. In contrast, the opposite of a matter of fact is conceivable in the mind, and thus matters of fact require *a posteriori* experience in order to verify whether they are true or not.

Applying Hume's fork to Descartes' trademark argument, we can see that premise 2 above is a matter of fact rather than a relation of ideas. This is because _____

_____

_____

_____ . This shows that the trademark argument _____

_____

_____ and thus fails to establish "God exists" *a priori*.

# The Limits of Knowledge

## What is local scepticism?    *(3 marks)*

Local scepticism is the belief that knowledge *within a particular area* is impossible.

For example, a person who is sceptical about _____

may believe any knowledge about _____

is impossible. Although someone may be a local sceptic within this area, they may

still believe that knowledge in other areas is possible (so not a global sceptic).

## Local or global scepticism? Cross out the wrong answer for each example.

| | |
|---|---|
| Belief that knowledge of God is impossible. | Global  /  Local |
| Belief that we cannot know about other people's minds. | Global  /  Local |
| Belief that we cannot know anything at all. | Global  /  Local |

## Philosophical scepticism or normal incredulity?

| | |
|---|---|
| Doubting whether you locked the door when you left. | Philosophical  /  Normal |
| Doubting whether you have hands because you might actually just be a brain in a vat. | Philosophical  /  Normal |
| Doubting whether you really did meet that person or whether you just dreamed you did. | Philosophical  /  Normal |
| Doubting whether you exist because your thoughts could just be disembodied illusions created by an evil demon. | Philosophical  /  Normal |
| Doubting whether the philosophy exam is on Tuesday. | Philosophical  /  Normal |
| Doubting whether aliens exist. | Philosophical  /  Normal |

## Outline the difference between philosophical scepticism and normal incredulity. *(5 marks)*

Normal incredulity is when we doubt a particular claim in everyday life. For example, I

may doubt my belief that _____

because _____

_____ . Doubt in the case of normal incredulity

can be removed by evidence. For example, if _____

_____

then I would no longer doubt this belief as it has been proved by evidence.

Philosophical scepticism, on the other hand, involves considering all possible reasons

to doubt a claim even if these reasons are unrealistic and impractical. For example, I

may doubt my belief that "I have hands" – even though I can see them – because of

sceptical scenarios such as _____ .

In this case, my doubt surrounding my belief that "I have hands" cannot be removed

by the evidence of my eyes because _____

_____ .

---

### ⑦ Multiple choice: Select the correct answer(s) from the boxes below.

Which **definition of knowledge** provides a potential response that defends ordinary knowledge against global scepticism?

☐ No false lemmas.

☐ Reliabilism.

☐ Infallibilism.

☐ Virtue epistemology.

<u>Missing words:</u> **justify, ideas, possible, evil demon, false, perceptions, deceiving, perceived**

Global scepticism is the belief that we cannot know anything at all. This belief is typically justified by sceptical scenarios and thought experiments, such as Descartes' _____ . In this scenario, an _____ is _____ me in every possible way. For example, all my _____ are illusions created by the _____ and even my basic reasoning abilities are being distorted by the _____ . So, in this scenario, all my beliefs would be _____ and I wouldn't know. Such a scenario is _____ and I am unable to prove it is _____ because my experience would be the same either way. As such, I cannot _____ my beliefs because I cannot _____ my belief that I'm not being deceived by an _____.

Berkeley's idealism is a theory of perception that says what we perceive are mind-dependent _____ . According to Berkeley, *"esse est percipi"*, which translates as *"to be is to be _____"*. In other words, _____ are reality according to idealism and there are no mind-independent objects.

If this theory of perception is correct, then global scepticism doesn't work. Sceptical scenarios describe situations where our _____ are somehow different to reality. For example, in Descartes' _____ scenario, reality is one way but the _____ is _____ us to make it seem that reality is somehow completely different. However, if *"to be is to be _____"*, as

Berkeley claims, then there is no such gap between _____ and reality.

As such, it is not _____ for sceptical scenarios to cast doubt on our

_____ and the knowledge gained from them.

## Does global scepticism succeed in demonstrating that all knowledge is impossible? (25 marks)

*Possible paragraph starters:*

**Introduction:** Global scepticism is the philosophical view that... In this essay I will defend global scepticism and argue that all knowledge is impossible because...

**Descartes' evil demon:** Descartes' method of doubt consists of three 'waves' of doubt. In the third wave of doubt, Descartes' considers the possibility that...

**Descartes' own responses:** Despite proposing the evil demon scenario initially, Descartes goes on to reject global scepticism and defend his ordinary knowledge. His first step in doing so is the cogito argument...

**Counter-response:** However, there are several steps in Descartes' responses that can be doubted, which takes us back to square 1: Scepticism. For example, ...

**Exam tip:**
Detailed explanations are key to hitting the top grade boundaries. Explain every step of each argument and **make logical links clear –** even if they seem obvious.

**Berkeley's response:** Berkeley's idealism argues that what we perceive are mind-dependent ideas... If this theory is correct, scepticism doesn't work because...

**Counter-response:** However, this response requires idealism is the correct theory of perception, but there are several conclusive objections to idealism, such as...

**Russell's response:** Rather than trying to deductively disprove scepticism, Russell takes an abductive approach, arguing that a mind-independent world is the best...

**Counter-response:** This response fails to adequately defeat scepticism, however, because both hypotheses – evil demon and mind-independent world – are equally compatible with our experiences. And so, this means we cannot justify...

**Conclusion:** In conclusion, global scepticism succeeds in showing all knowledge...

# Epistemology Crossword Puzzle

# Clues

## Across

[2] The name for Berkeley's argument that attempts to show mind-independent objects are inconceivable and impossible.

[4] Something that is true in every possible world and couldn't be false.

[5] Something that is true in this world but could have been false in another possible world.

[8] Knowledge that does not require experience of the external world to be known.

[9] The name of Descartes' argument that "I exist".

[13] The theory of perception which says we perceive mind-independent objects indirectly via sense data.

[18] Knowledge that require experience of the external world to be known.

[19] The definition of knowledge that requires a belief to be impossible to rationally doubt.

[21] The theory of perception which says we perceive mind-dependent ideas and that a mind-independent objects don't exist.

[22] The form of scepticism that says knowledge within a particular area is impossible.

## Down

[1] The name of the philosopher who came up with the counterexample to the justified true belief definition of knowledge.

[3] The use of logically valid reasoning to derive true propositions from other true propositions.

[6] The name for the definition of knowledge as justified true belief.

[7] The type of knowledge that is knowledge of facts.

[10] The owner of the slave in Plato's 'slave boy' argument for innate knowledge.

[11] The theory of perception which says we perceive mind-independent objects and their properties directly.

[12] The belief that human beings are born with innate propositional knowledge.

[14] The belief that all (or at least most) knowledge comes from experience.

[15] A statement that is true in virtue of how the world is.

[16] A statement that is true in virtue of the meaning of the words.

[17] The definition of knowledge that provides a response to global scepticism.

[20] The form of scepticism that says all knowledge is impossible.

# Epistemology Practice Questions

## 3 mark questions

Define 1. Ability knowledge, 2. Acquaintance knowledge, and 3. Propositional knowledge. (3 marks)

What is the tripartite definition of knowledge? (3 marks)

What is the no false lemmas definition of knowledge? (3 marks)

What is infallibilism? (3 marks)

What is reliabilism? (3 marks)

What is virtue epistemology? (3 marks)

What is direct realism? (3 marks)

What is indirect realism? (3 marks)

What is idealism? (3 marks)

What is *a priori* knowledge? (3 marks)

What is *a posteriori* knowledge? (3 marks)

What is an analytic truth? (3 marks)

What is a synthetic truth? (3 marks)

What is a necessary truth? (3 marks)

What is a contingent truth? (3 marks)

Briefly outline what Descartes means by a 'clear and distinct idea'. (3 marks)

Briefly outline the intuition and deduction thesis. (3 marks)

What is innatism? (3 marks)

What is empiricism? (3 marks)

What is philosophical scepticism? (3 marks)

What is normal incredulity? (3 marks)

What is local scepticism? (3 marks)

What is global scepticism? (3 marks)

## 5 mark questions

Outline the view that 'belief' is not a necessary condition of knowledge. (5 marks)

How does adding a 'no false lemmas' condition to the tripartite definition of knowledge avoid Gettier cases? (5 marks)

Explain how reliabilism differs from virtue epistemology. (5 marks)

Explain how hallucinations present an issue for direct realism. (5 marks)

Explain how the time lag argument presents an issue for direct realism. (5 marks)

Explain how perceptual variation presents an issue for direct realism. (5 marks)

Outline Locke's primary/secondary quality distinction. (5 marks)

Explain how indirect realism leads to scepticism about the existence of mind-independent objects. (5 marks)

Outline Berkeley's 'master argument' for idealism. (5 marks)

Explain the objection that Berkeley's idealism leads to solipsism. (5 marks)

Explain how the role of God could be an issue for Berkeley's idealism. (5 marks)

What is Plato trying to show about knowledge in his Meno's slave argument? (5 marks)

Explain Locke's view that the mind is a 'tabula rasa' at birth. (5 marks)

What is Hume's Fork? (5 marks)

Outline Descartes' third wave of doubt. (5 marks)

Outline Descartes' cogito argument. (5 marks)

Outline the role of philosophical scepticism within epistemology. (5 marks)

Explain how philosophical scepticism differs from normal incredulity. (5 marks)


## 12 mark questions

Outline the tripartite definition of knowledge and explain how one of Gettier's original counterexamples attacks this definition. (12 marks)

Explain how virtue epistemology could show that Smith lacks knowledge in one of Gettier's original counterexamples. (12 marks)

Briefly explain direct realism and explain how perceptual variation could challenge this view. (12 marks)

Outline indirect realism and explain Berkeley's objection that mind-dependent sense data cannot be like mind-independent objects. (12 marks)

Outline how indirect realism leads to scepticism about the existence of mind-independent objects and explain Russell's response that mind-independent objects are the best hypothesis. (12 marks)

Explain Leibniz's argument that knowledge of necessary truths is innate. (12 marks)

Explain Locke's arguments against innatism. (12 marks)

Outline Descartes' three waves of doubt and explain the role of philosophical scepticism within epistemology.  (12 marks)

Briefly outline Descartes' proof of the external world and explain how Hume's fork could be applied to this argument. (12 marks)

Explain how reliabilism could provide a response to philosophical scepticism. (12 marks)

Outline philosophical scepticism and explain how Berkeley's idealism could provide a response that defends ordinary knowledge. (12 marks)


## 25 mark questions

How should propositional knowledge be defined? (25 marks)

Assess direct realism. (25 marks)

Is indirect realism convincing? (25 marks)

Is Berkeley's idealism a plausible theory of perception? (25 marks)

Is the mind at birth a 'tabula rasa', as Locke claims? (25 marks)

To what extent can knowledge be acquired using *a priori* intuition and deduction? (25 marks)

Is global scepticism correct to say all knowledge is impossible? (25 marks)

# Answers

*Note: Many of the answers below are not the only correct possible answers, but simply suggestions of what could be written in the blank spaces.*

Page 7:

**Outline the tripartite definition of knowledge and explain how Gettier cases challenge this definition. (12 marks)**

1. *Justified,*   2. *True,*   3. *Belief.*

"...conditions are both necessary and *sufficient* for knowledge"

"...overhears the interviewer say *"I'm going to give Jones the job."*

"...Smith forms the belief that *"the man who will get the job has 10 coins in his pocket."*

"...Smith's *belief* that *"the man who will get the job has 10 coins in his pocket"* was *justified* and *true* and therefore..."

"...they are not a *sufficient* definition of knowledge."

Page 8:

**How does adding a 'no false lemmas' condition to the tripartite definition of knowledge avoid Gettier cases? (5 marks)**

"...Smith's belief that *"Jones will get the job"* when, in reality,..."

"...Smith's belief here is true and *justified* so meets all 3 conditions of..."

"...it does not count as knowledge *it was just a lucky coincidence that Smith also had 10 coins in his pocket.*"

"...derived from the false lemma that *Jones will get the job.*"

Page 9:

**Match the definition of knowledge (left) to its description (right).**

1= D,  2 = C,  3 = A,  4 = B

**Match the type of knowledge (left) to its description (right).**

1= C,  2 = A,  3 = B

**Which of the following are examples of intellectual virtues?**

*Being open-minded,  caring about evidence,  caring about the truth,  being rational*

**Fake Barn County is an issue for which definition(s) of knowledge?**

*Justified true belief,  no false lemmas,  reliabilism*

Page 10:

**What is reliabilism? (3 marks)**

"...1. P is *true*..."

"...2. S *believes* that P..."

"...3. S's *belief* that P is formed via a *reliable* method."

**What is ability knowledge? (3 marks)**

"...For example, *knowing how to ride a bicycle...*" or "...For example, *knowing how to juggle...*", etc.

**What is virtue epistemology? (3 marks)**

"...Virtue epistemology definitions of knowledge invoke *intellectual* virtues,..." or "...invoke *epistemic* virtues,..."

"...such as being rational and *unbiased.*" or "...such as being rational and *open-minded.*", etc.

"...successfully using their *intellectual* virtues,..." or "...successfully using their *epistemic* virtues,..."

Page 11:

**What is infallibilism? (3 marks)**

"...justified in such a way that they are *certain* (i.e. impossible to doubt)."

"...due to sceptical scenarios such as *the evil demon*..." or "...due to sceptical scenarios such as *brain in a vat*...", etc.

**How should propositional knowledge be defined? (25 marks)**

"...not acquaintance or *ability* knowledge."

**Fake Barn County objection to no false lemmas definition of knowledge**

"...In Fake Barn County _the locals create fake barn facades that look just like real barns_."

"...his belief is false because _he's looking at the fake barns_."

"...this time it is 1. _Justified_ 2. _True_ and 3. _Not inferred from a false lemma_."

"...it is not really knowledge because _it's just lucky that he happened to be looking at the one real barn_."

"...shows that the no false lemmas definition of knowledge is not a _sufficient_ definition of knowledge..."

**Outline the argument from illusion against direct realism. (5 marks)**

"Direct realism is the claim that what we perceive are mind- _independent_ objects and their properties."

"...in cases of illusion what we are perceiving is not a mind- _independent_ object or a property of it."

"For example, a stick may look _crooked_ to us when in water..." or "For example, a stick may look _bent_ to us when in water..."

"...but in reality it does not have the property of being _crooked_." or "...but in reality it does not have the property of being _bent_."

"This shows that our _perception_ of the stick..."

"...is different from the mind- _independent_ reality of the stick..."

"...and so what we are perceiving is not a mind- _independent_ object or its properties..."

**Explain how Berkeley's idealism differs from indirect realism. (5 marks)**

"...Indirect realism says _a mind-independent external world does exist_ (so is a _realist_ theory)..."

"...whereas idealism says _a mind-independent external world does not exist_ (so is an _anti-realist_ theory)..."

"...idealism is a _direct_ theory of perception because it says _mind-dependent ideas are reality and we perceive these ideas directly_ ..."

"...whereas idealism says we perceive (mind-independent) reality _indirectly_ via _sense data._"

**Outline the argument that indirect realism leads to scepticism about the existence of mind-independent objects and explain Russell's response that the external world is the best hypothesis. (12 marks)**

_mind-independent, indirectly, sense data, sense data, mind-dependent, mind-independent, justify, scepticism, mind-independent, mind-independent, mind-independent, hypothesis, abductive, mind-independent, mind-independent, perceiving, perceiving, perceiving, mind-independent, mind-dependent_

"...and so _we should believe in the existence of mind-independent objects_." or "...and so _is the best hypothesis to explain our perceptions_."

**Outline Berkeley's 'master argument' for idealism. (5 marks)**

"Berkeley's idealism is the view that _mind-independent objects do not exist and instead what we perceive are mind-dependent ideas._"

"...Philonous asks Hylas to conceive of a tree that _is not being perceived by anyone._"

"...Philonous responds to this and says that the tree Hylas is imagining cannot be mind-_independent_ at all..."

"...Berkeley takes this to show that mind-_independent_ objects are _inconceivable_..."

"...If mind-_independent_ objects are impossible, then everything must be mind-_dependent_ and thus idealism is correct."

**According to indirect realism, what are the immediate objects of perception?**

_Mind-dependent sense data._

**Match the theory of perception (left) to its description (right).**

1= C, 2 = A, 3 = B

**Which of the following are arguments against direct realism?**

_Perceptual variation, Time lag, Hallucination._

**Which of the following are arguments against Berkeley's idealism?**

_Illusion, Hallucination, God doesn't change but perceptions do, Solipsism_

**Relational properties response to perceptual variation objection to direct realism**

"...relational properties can defend the direct realist's claim that what we perceive are mind-_independent_ objects and their properties."

"...The same reasoning can be applied to cases of perceptual variation. For example, _it is possible for a table to have both the (mind-independent) relational property of looking square relative to a perceiver who is directly above the table whilst simultaneously having the (mind-independent) relational property of looking diamond-shaped relative to a perceiver who is looking at the table from an angle_."

"...This shows that perceptual variation does not disprove direct realism because _in the case of both perceptions (a square-shaped table and a diamond-shaped table) what we are perceiving is still a mind-independent object and its (relational) properties. The mind-independent object itself doesn't change_."

## Page 21:

**What is an analytic truth? (3 marks)**

"An analytic truth is something that is _true in virtue of the meaning of the words…_"

"...For example, _"a bachelor is an unmarried man" is an analytic truth_."

**What is _a posteriori_ knowledge? (3 marks)**

"_A posteriori_ knowledge is _knowledge that requires experience of the external world before it can be known_…"

"...For example, _"Paris is the capital of France" requires experience to verify (e.g. looking at a map) and so is a posteriori_."

## Page 22:

**Which of the following are arguments for innate knowledge?**

_Meno's slave, Leibniz's argument from necessary truths_

**Which of the following are contingent truths?**

_Grass is green, Paris is the capital of France_

**Which of the following sources of knowledge are a priori?**

_Rational intuition, Logical deduction_

**Which of the following does rationalism claim?**

_Some knowledge of synthetic truths can come from a priori intuition and deduction._

## Page 23:

**Outline innatism and explain how Leibniz's argument based on necessary truths supports this view. (12 marks)**

"Innatism is the view that _human beings are born already possessing some innate (propositional) knowledge…_"

"...In contrast, _contingent_ truths are true but could have been false…"

"...For example, _"Paris is the capital of France"_ ." or "...For example, _"grass is green"_ .", etc.

"...Leibniz takes this to demonstrate innate knowledge because _experience can only tell us what is contingently true in specific instances, and yet we have knowledge that necessary truths must always be true (in every possible world). Since this knowledge can't come from experience, Leibniz concludes that it is innate_."

## Page 26:

**Outline the meaning of 'intuition' and 'deduction' within Descartes' approach to gaining knowledge. (5 marks)**

"Intuition and deduction are _a priori_ methods of gaining knowledge…"

"...intuition is the ability of the mind to see "_clear_ and _distinct_ ideas" are true…"

"...An example of this is his _cogito_ argument, …"

"Deduction is the use of deductively _valid_ reasoning to derive…"

**In _Meditations_, which 3 synthetic truths does Descartes attempt to prove by using a priori intuition and deduction?**

_I exist, God exists, The external world exists_

**Match the argument (left) to its conclusion (right).**

1= B, 2 = D, 3 = A, 4 = C

## Page 27:

**Briefly explain Hume's fork. (5 marks)**

"...judgements of reason: 1. Relations of _ideas_ , and 2. Matters of _fact_…"

"...The key feature of a relation of _ideas_ is that it _cannot_ be denied without leading to a _contradiction_…"

"...For example, "triangles have 3 sides" is a relation of _ideas_ because _the idea of a 4-sided triangle is self-contradictory and thus inconceivable to the mind_…"

"...Relations of _ideas_ can thus be known purely _a priori_."

"...The key feature of a matter of _fact_ is that it _can_ be denied without leading to a _contradiction_..."

"...For example, even though "grass is green" is true, it's logically possible _that grass could be red or some other colour. We can conceive of red grass without contradiction_..."

"...in order to know a matter of _fact_, we require empirical experience and thus matters of _fact_ can only be known _a posteriori_."

**What is empiricism? (3 marks)**

"Empiricism is the view that all (or at least most) knowledge comes from _experience..._"

"...and so all knowledge is _a posteriori_..."

"...reject the claim of rationalist philosophers that _a priori_ reasoning methods (such as _intuition_ and deduction) alone..."

"...can establish knowledge of _synthetic_ truths."

## Page 29:

**Briefly explain Descartes' trademark argument for the existence of God and explain how Hume's fork might be applied to this argument. (12 marks)**

"...This is because _we can conceive of a cause of an effect that has less reality than the effect without leading to contradiction_..."

"...This shows that the trademark argument _relies on a posteriori matters of fact rather than only a priori intuition and deduction_ and thus fails to establish "God exists" _a priori_."

## Page 30:

**What is local scepticism? (3 marks)**

"...For example, a person who is sceptical about _morality_ may believe any knowledge about _moral facts and properties_ is impossible..."
or

"...For example, a person who is sceptical about _the future_ may believe any knowledge about _the future_ is impossible..."
or

"...For example, a person who is sceptical about _religion_ may believe any knowledge about _God's existence and character_ is impossible..."
etc.

**Local or global scepticism?**
Belief that knowledge of God is impossible. = Local
Belief that we cannot know about other people's minds. = Local
Belief that we cannot know anything at all. = Global

**Philosophical scepticism or normal incredulity?**
Doubting whether you locked the door when you left. = Normal
Doubting whether you have hands because you might actually just be a brain in a vat. = Philosophical
Doubting whether you really did meet that person or whether you just dreamed you did. = Normal
Doubting whether you exist because your thoughts could just be disembodied illusions created by an evil demon. = Philosophical
Doubting whether the philosophy exam is on Tuesday. = Normal
Doubting whether aliens exist. = Normal

## Page 31:

**Outline the difference between philosophical scepticism and normal incredulity. (5 marks)**

"...For example, I may doubt my belief that _I locked the door when I left the house_ because _I can't remember locking the door when I left_. Doubt in the case of normal incredulity can be removed by evidence. For example, if _I went home and checked and saw that my door was locked_ then I would no longer doubt..." etc.

"...I may doubt my belief that "I have hands" – even though I can see them – because of sceptical scenarios such as _Descartes' evil demon_. In this case, my doubt surrounding my belief that "I have hands" cannot be removed by the evidence of my eyes because _the evil demon could be tricking me into perceiving that I have hands when in reality I don't and my perception would be exactly the same as if I really did have hands_." etc.

**Which definition of knowledge provides a potential response that defends ordinary knowledge against global scepticism?**
_Reliabilism._

## Page 32:

**Outline global scepticism and explain how Berkeley's idealism could be applied as a response. (12 marks)**

_evil demon, evil demon, deceiving, perceptions, evil demon, evil demon, false, possible, false, justify, justify, evil demon, ideas, perceived, perceptions, perceptions, evil demon, evil demon, deceiving, perceived, perceptions, possible, perceptions_

Epistemology – Answers

**Epistemology crossword puzzle**

| Across | Down |
|---|---|
| [2] MASTER | [1] GETTIER |
| [4] NECESSARY | [3] DEDUCTION |
| [5] CONTINGENT | [6] TRIPARTITE |
| [8] APRIORI | [7] PROPOSITIONAL |
| [9] COGITO | [10] MENO |
| [13] INDIRECTREALISM | [11] DIRECTREALISM |
| [18] APOSTERIORI | [12] INNATISM |
| [19] INFALLIBILISM | [14] EMPIRICISM |
| [21] IDEALISM | [15] SYNTHETIC |
| [22] LOCAL | [16] ANALYTIC |
| | [17] RELIABILISM |
| | [20] GLOBAL |

# Moral Philosophy

## Utilitarianism

---

**(?) Multiple choice: Select the correct answer(s) from the boxes below.**

Which of the following is **not** a feature of **act utilitarianism**?

☐ Hedonistic.                    ☐ Consequentialist.

☐ Agent-centred.                 ☐ Action-centred.

---

**→ Match the type of utilitarianism (left) to its description (right).**

1. Act            A. We should maximise people's *preferences*, not pleasures

2. Rule           B. We should maximise pleasure *in each specific instance*

3. Preference     C. We should follow *general laws* that maximise pleasure

---

**(?) Multiple choice: Select the correct answer(s) from the boxes below.**

Which of the following forms of utilitarianism takes a ***qualitative* approach**?

☐ Bentham's act utilitarianism.          ☐ Rule utilitarianism.

☐ Mill's higher and lower pleasures.     ☐ Preference utilitarianism.

---

**(?) Multiple choice: Select the correct answer(s) from the boxes below.**

Which philosopher created the **felicific calculus** (AKA the utility calculus)?

☐ Peter Singer.                  ☐ John Stuart Mill.

☐ Jeremy Bentham.                ☐ Robert Nozick.

## What is preference utilitarianism? *(3 marks)*

**Cross out the wrong answers below, leaving the correct descriptions.**

Preference utilitarianism is a _hedonistic / non-hedonistic_ ethical theory which says that an act is morally right if it maximises satisfaction of people's _preferences / pleasures_. It is a _consequentialist / non-consequentialist_ ethical theory.

## Outline Nozick's experience machine thought experiment and explain how this could be used as a criticism of utilitarianism. *(5 marks)*

The **PEEL** structure (see page 12) can also be an effective way to structure answers to some of the shorter questions. Finish the answer below by *explaining* what the example shows and *linking* it back to what the question asks.

**Point:** Hedonistic forms of utilitarianism say that goodness/moral value boils down to pleasure. However, the experience machine illustrates there are other moral values.

**~~Evidence/Example:~~** In the experience machine thought experiment, a person can plug into a machine that provides them with all the pleasurable experiences they want. This life would be far more pleasurable than life in the real world.

**Explanation:** However, many people would prefer to remain in the real world than to enter the experience machine. For example, a reason someone may prefer to live in the real world is _____

_____ .

**Link:** This is a problem for (hedonistic) utilitarianism because _____

_____

_____ .

***You're the examiner!*** **Use the mark scheme below to mark the example answers.**

| 5/5 | A full, clear and precise explanation. The student makes logical links between precisely identified points, with no redundancy. |
|---|---|
| 4/5 | A clear explanation, with logical links, but some imprecision/redundancy. |
| 3/5 | The substantive content of the explanation is present and there is an attempt at logical linking, but the explanation is not full and/or precise. |
| 2/5 | One or two relevant points made, but not precisely. The logic is unclear. |
| 1/5 | Fragmented points, with no logical structure. |
| 0/5 | Nothing written worthy of credit. |

If most people want something but one person doesn't then utilitarianism says we should do it because that's what most people want. But this might not be fair.

 _____ / 5

According to utilitarianism, an action is morally right if it creates the greatest pleasure for the greatest number of people. However, there are scenarios where the act that creates the greatest pleasure is morally wrong. For example, if 10,000 people got 1 unit of pleasure from seeing an innocent person be tortured, and the person being tortured suffered 100 units of pain, then torturing the innocent person would result in the greatest pleasure (because 10,000 > 100). Thus, utilitarianism would say torturing the innocent person is the right thing to do. However, it is morally wrong – regardless of the consequences – to torture an innocent person. This shows that utilitarianism can lead to morally incorrect outcomes in certain situations.

 _____ / 5

## Outline Mill's qualitative hedonistic utilitarianism (higher and lower pleasures). *(5 marks)*

Hedonistic forms of utilitarianism claim that _____ is the source of moral worth (i.e. _____ = good). However, Mill's qualitative hedonistic utilitarianism distinguishes between the 'higher' pleasures of the mind and the 'lower' pleasures of the body. An example of a 'higher' pleasure would be

_____

whereas an example of a 'lower' pleasure would be _____

_____ . Mill argues that anyone who has experienced both 'higher' and 'lower' pleasures will always prefer the former over the latter and that 'higher' pleasures are better and more valuable than 'lower' pleasures.

## Outline Mill's 'proof' of the greatest happiness principle.    *(5 marks)*

**The steps of the argument below are in the wrong order. Using the spaces provided, number them from 1-5 so they are in the correct order.**

\# _____  All other things humans value – for example, virtue – they value *because* they increase happiness.

\# _____  The *desirability* of happiness is "all the proof which the case admits of" that happiness is a *good*.

\# __5__  So, not only is happiness *a* good, it is the *only* good.

\# _____  The only proof that something is *desirable* is that people desire it.

\# _____  Each person desires their own happiness, therefore the general happiness is *desirable*.

<u>Missing words:</u> **dogs, quantify, equally, propinquity, pleasure, fecundity, impractical, purity**

According to quantitative hedonistic utilitarianism, an act is morally good if it results in more _____ than pain. The more _____ that results from an act, the more morally valuable it is. Bentham's utility calculus is a way to _____ the _____ that results from an act, and therefore _____ how morally good it is. The calculus has seven variables: Intensity, duration, certainty, _____ , _____ , _____ , and extent. If we have two courses of action, A and B, we apply the utility calculus to both A and B and whichever course of action results in the greater quantity of _____ is the morally correct one.

A criticism of the utility calculus and of quantitative hedonistic utilitarianism in general is that it is difficult to calculate in practice. For example, it is unclear how to _____ each of the seven variables as _____ and pain cannot easily be measured without tools such as brain scanners. Further, even if one were able to _____ the intensity of a _____ , one would not be able to measure the _____ of that action (i.e. how likely that action is to result in more _____ ) because this would have to involve predicting the future. For example, saving someone's life may result in more short-term _____ , but if that person went on to become a serial killer then the utility calculus may instead suggest it is better to let that person die.

These difficulties in calculation are further compounded by the question of which beings to include. For example, _____ can feel _____ and pain just like human beings can, which raises the question of whether we should include them in our utility calculus. And if we are to include _____ in our calculation, this raises the further question of whether their _____ and pain should be treated _____ to human beings. The issue is that these calculations are massively _____ , if not impossible, to carry out in practice each time one is faced with a moral choice.

## Is utilitarianism a convincing account of morality? *(25 marks)*

*Possible paragraph starters:*

**Introduction:** Utilitarianism is a consequentialist normative ethical theory... I will argue that no form of utilitarianism provides a convincing account of morality...

**Utility calculus:** Quantitative hedonistic utilitarianism says... Bentham's utility calculus...

**Difficulties with calculation response:** However, an issue with the utility calculus is that it is difficult, if not impossible, to calculate in practice....

**Counter-response (rule utilitarianism):** Rule utilitarianism avoids this issue as it does not require us to calculate the utility of each individual act...

**Response to rule utilitarianism:** However, rule utilitarianism faces its own problems, such as....

**Exam tip:**
Using the **different types of utilitarianism** is a great way to respond to criticisms and ensure your essay is balanced whilst showing detailed understanding.

**Nozick's experience machine:** A further issue for hedonistic forms of utilitarianism is...

**Response (preference utilitarianism):** Preference utilitarianism avoids this issue by...

**Counter-response (conflicting preferences):** However, this raises the issue of...

**Conclusion:** In conclusion, all forms of utilitarianism are unconvincing...

# Kantian Deontological Ethics

(?) **Multiple choice: Select the correct answer(s) from the boxes below.**

Why would Kant say we have a **perfect duty never to tell lies**?

☐ It makes the person unhappy when they realise they've been lied to.

☐ Telling lies leads to a contradiction in conception when universalised.

☐ Telling lies leads to a contradiction in will when universalised.

☐ Telling lies will lead you to develop bad character.

(?) **Categorical or hypothetical imperative? Cross out the wrong answer for each example.**

| | |
|---|---|
| Don't steal. | Categorical / Hypothetical |
| Don't steal if you don't want to break the law. | Categorical / Hypothetical |
| You should leave now if you want to get there on time. | Categorical / Hypothetical |
| You shouldn't eat animals. | Categorical / Hypothetical |
| If you want people to trust you, don't lie. | Categorical / Hypothetical |
| Don't lie. | Categorical / Hypothetical |

(?) **Multiple choice: Select the correct answer(s) from the boxes below.**

Which of the following are **issues** for Kant's deontological ethics?

☐ Ignores consequences.          ☐ Competing duties.

☐ Tyranny of the majority.          ☐ Circularity.

☐ Ignores other valuable motivations.          ☐ Ignores duties to our family/friends.

## Explain Kant's first formulation of the categorical imperative. (5 marks)

The first formulation of the categorical imperative says to "act only according to that

_____ whereby you can at the same time will it should become a

universal law without contradiction". In other words, it is morally wrong to follow a

rule that leads to a contradiction. Kant gives two types of contradictions that can

result from an action: Contradiction in _____ and contradiction in

_____ . A maxim leads to a contradiction in _____ if it

would be *self-contradictory* for everybody to follow it, resulting in a _____

duty *not* to follow that maxim. A maxim leads to a contradiction in _____

if it contradicts something we must *rationally will*, resulting in an _____

duty to follow that maxim (at least some of the time).

## Explain the distinction between acting out of duty and acting in accordance with duty. (5 marks)

**Cross out the wrong answers below, leaving the correct descriptions.**

According to Kant, our duty is to follow the moral law. To act *in accordance with / out of*

duty is to behave in line with this moral law (for example, because we want to)

whereas to act *in accordance with / out of* duty is to choose to act in line with the moral

law *because* it is the moral law and the right thing to do. For example, a shopkeeper

who does not rip off their customers in order to keep a good reputation acts *in*

*accordance with / out of* duty, but a shopkeeper who does not rip off their customers

because doing so would be morally wrong acts *in accordance with / out of* duty.

## What is the humanity formula?        (3 marks)

The humanity formula is the second formulation of Kant's categorical imperative. It says to never treat humans as _____ but always as _____ in themselves. This is because all human beings have autonomy and rational agency to pursue their own _____ .

## Explain the objection to Kant's deontological ethics that not all universalisable maxims are moral.        (5 marks)

According to Kant's deontological ethics, actions/maxims that cannot be _____ are morally wrong whereas actions/maxims that can be _____ are morally permissible. However, there are several examples of maxims that are morally wrong and yet can be _____ .

For example, the maxim "to steal" cannot be _____ without leading to a contradiction in _____ because if it was always OK to steal, private property wouldn't exist. However, if we say the maxim is "to steal from shops beginning with the letter A", this maxim can be _____ without leading to a contradiction in _____ because it would apply in such a narrow range of situations that the concept of private property would still be coherent. However, it is morally wrong to steal – regardless of whether the shop's name begins with the letter A – and yet this maxim can be _____ .

This shows that _____

_____

_____ .

**Outline what Kant means by the 'good will' and explain the objection that this ignores the value of other motivations.** *(12 marks)*

 Missing words: friendship, qualification, consequences, duty, love

According to Kant, good will means to act for the sake of _____ . This means to choose our actions because of _____ and not for some other reason, such as the _____ of that action or our own personal goals and desires. Kant further says that good will is the only thing that is good without _____ and is the source of moral worth.

An issue with Kant's account here is that there are other motivations that are morally valuable besides _____ , such as _____ and _____ .

For example, if a father — Father A — does not enjoy spending time with his children and playing with them but does so anyway because he has a _____ to do so, then this father's actions *do* have moral worth according to Kant. However, if a different Father — Father B — spends time with his children and spends time playing with them out of _____ and because he genuinely enjoys doing so, this action does *not* have moral worth according to Kant because Father B's actions are not chosen because of _____ .

The objection is that Father B's motivation — the _____ for his children — *does* have moral worth and is in fact even more morally valuable than Father A's motivation. However, Kant's theory says the opposite. This shows that Kant's claim that the good will is the only morally valuable motivation is false, as there are other valuable motivations, such as _____ and _____ .

## Outline Philippa Foot's objection to Kant's deontological ethics that morality is a system of hypothetical, not categorical, imperatives. *(12 marks)*

🧩 <u>Missing words:</u> **etiquette, ends, villainy, motivation, hypothetical, contradictions, irrational, categorical, maxims, inconsistency**

A _____ imperative is an instruction that applies to all people at all times regardless of personal circumstances. In contrast, a _____ imperative only applies to people who have particular goals/ends. According to Kant, moral imperatives such as "don't steal" are _____ and so apply to all people at all times. However, Foot argues that Kant does not provide adequate reason why this is the case and instead morality should be understood as a system of _____ imperatives.

Kant claims that it is _____ to act on maxims such as "don't steal" because they lead to _____ when universalised. However, Foot argues that there is nothing _____ about acting on this maxim if you never accepted it in the first place. Such a person can be convicted of _____ but not _____ , she says. Further, although we may feel that the rules of morality bind us in a way that is _____ , that feeling is just that: A feeling. In reality, there is no _____ reason that forces us to follow the rules of morality any more than there is a _____ reason to follow the rules of _____ .

Instead, Foot argues that moral rules should be understood as _____ imperatives where people only have reason to follow moral rules *if they have the relevant moral* _____ *or goals*. For example, the maxim "don't steal" could be  understood as "don't steal *if you care about justice and property rights.*"

This maxim would only apply to people who care about justice and property rights.

However, this care for these values provides _____ to follow this moral

imperative in a way Kant's _____ imperative does not.

## Assess Kant's deontological ethics. *(25 marks)*

*Possible paragraph starters:*

**Introduction:** ...In this essay I will argue Kant's account is a poor account of morality.

**Categorical imperative:** Kant's deontological ethics centres on the categorical imperative, which says... For example, the maxim "to steal" fails the categorical imperative because...

**Not all universalisable maxims are moral:** However, an issue for the categorical imperative is that we can justify immoral actions by defining our maxims cleverly. In the stealing example, I could say my maxim is "to steal from shops beginning with the letter A on Wednesdays", in which case...

**Kant's response:** Kant would respond that the categorical imperative must be applied to my actual maxim and that the name of the shop and day of the week are irrelevant...

**Response to Kant:** A stronger counter-example is the maxim "to steal in order to save a life". This maxim can be universalised and the extra details are morally relevant...

**Ignores consequences:** A further issue for Kant's deontological ethics is that it ignores the moral value of consequences. For example, if a would-be murderer asks you where their victim is, ...

**Kant's response:** In response, Kant argues the good will is the source of moral value, not consequences...

**Response to Kant:** However, a stronger counter-example illustrates how absurd Kant's theory is. If someone had a bomb that would blow up the entire universe and said "tell a lie or I'll detonate it"...

**Exam tip:**
You don't have to cover *every* argument on the syllabus for the 25 mark questions. Pick two or three issues or arguments and cover those **in detail**.

**Conclusion:** In conclusion, Kant's deontological ethics is a poor account of morality because...

# Aristotelian Virtue Ethics

➡️ **Match the Aristotelian term (left) to its English translation (right).**

| | | |
|---|---|---|
| 1. Eudaimonia | A. Practical wisdom |
| 2. Arête | B. Human flourishing, living and faring well |
| 3. Ergon | C. A property/trait that helps something fulfil its function |
| 4. Phronesis | D. The function/characteristic activity of something |

❓ **Multiple choice: Select the correct answer(s) from the boxes below.**

According to Aristotle, what is the unique **function** of human beings?

☐ To acquire wealth.   ☐ To be happy.

☐ To use reason.   ☐ To do philosophy.

❓ **Multiple choice: Select the correct answer(s) from the boxes below.**

According to Aristotle, which of the following is the **final end** for human beings?

☐ Pleasure.   ☐ Virtue.

☐ Eudaimonia.   ☐ Honour.

✏️ **Fill in the missing spaces in the table below.**

| Vice of deficiency | Virtue | Vice of excess |
|---|---|---|
| Cowardice | _____ | Recklessness |
| _____ | Modest | Shameless |
| Self-denial | Temperance | _____ |

**Outline Aristotle's account of how we develop moral character and explain the issue that his definition of 'virtuous acts' is circular.** *(12 marks)*

Missing words: **skill, role models, temperance, character, habits, virtues**

Moral character, for Aristotle, means possessing _____ such as courage and _____ . One is not born with these _____ but instead develops them over time, like learning a _____ . In the same way that someone learns a _____ by practising, a person learns _____ by acting virtuously. Acting in a virtuous way repeatedly over time creates _____ which become part of one's _____ . So, virtuous acts create virtuous _____ .

Aristotle defines virtuous acts as those that would be done by people who possess virtuous _____ and Aristotle defines people who possess virtuous _____ as those who are disposed to perform virtuous acts. However, if someone did not already know what virtuous _____ looked like, this definition would not help them understand what virtuous acts are. This is because the definition of virtuous acts contains the original term being defined. Similarly, if someone did not already know what virtuous acts are, this definition would not help them understand what virtuous _____ looks like because virtuous _____ is defined in terms of virtuous acts.

If someone is unable to understand what virtuous acts are, then they are unable to understand whether their actions and _____ are creating virtuous _____ . Further, if someone is unable to understand what virtuous _____ looks like, then they will not be able to identify virtuous _____ in order to understand what virtuous acts are and imitate them.

The issue is that the theory requires one to perform virtuous acts in order to develop virtuous _____ , but the circularity of these definitions suggest it would be impossible to learn what these terms mean in order to do so.

## Briefly outline how clashing/competing virtues may present an issue for Aristotelian virtue ethics.    (5 marks)

Aristotelian virtue ethics requires that we act virtuously, but in some circumstances one virtue may suggest one course of action and another virtue may suggest a contradictory course of action. For example, a judge who is sentencing a thief could choose to act in accordance with the virtue of _____ and sentence the thief or act in accordance with the virtue of _____ and let the thief go. However, the judge cannot do both actions and so whichever course of action the judge takes they will neglect a virtue and thus fail to act virtuously. This is an issue for Aristotelian virtue ethics because _____

_____

_____ .

## What is eudaimonia?    (3 marks)

In Aristotelian virtue ethics, eudaimonia translates as _____

_____ . It is the _____ end

for humans, meaning the thing for which everything else in life is done.

**Explain the objection that Aristotle's virtue ethics does not provide clear guidance for how to act.** *(5 marks)*

As an _____-centred moral theory, Aristotelian virtue ethics does not

provide a list of rules for morally correct actions. Instead, the theory requires that we

act how a _____ person would act. However, if one does not know how

a _____ person would act, this does not provide clear guidance for

behaviour. The doctrine of the _____ describes virtues as not too

much (a vice of _____ ) or too little (a vice of _____ )

but 'too much' and 'too little' are not actual amounts so this does not provide clear

guidance either. In contrast, _____-centred moral theories, such as

utilitarianism and Kantian deontological ethics prescribe specific actions. The issue

is that if faced with a genuine moral dilemma, such as _____

_____ ,

Aristotle's virtue ethics is not practically useful in deciding what is morally right to do.

---

**? Moral responsibility: Voluntary, involuntary, or non-voluntary action? Cross out the wrong answers for each example.**

Sailors throwing cargo overboard in a storm to avoid their ship sinking.

| Voluntary / Involuntary / Non-voluntary

A sailor throwing cargo overboard because he's had a bad day and is angry.

| Voluntary / Involuntary / Non-voluntary

A sailor mistakes some cargo for rubbish and mistakenly throws it overboard.

| Voluntary / Involuntary / Non-voluntary

**You're the examiner!** Use the mark scheme below to mark the example answers.

| | |
|---|---|
| **5/5** | A full, clear and precise explanation. The student makes logical links between precisely identified points, with no redundancy. |
| **4/5** | A clear explanation, with logical links, but some imprecision/redundancy. |
| **3/5** | The substantive content of the explanation is present and there is an attempt at logical linking, but the explanation is not full and/or precise. |
| **2/5** | One or two relevant points made, but not precisely. The logic is unclear. |
| **1/5** | Fragmented points, with no logical structure. |
| **0/5** | Nothing written worthy of credit. |

Aristotle says virtue is practical wisdom. The skill analogy compares learning virtue to learning a skill, such as playing a musical instrument. Practical wisdom means knowing how to act virtuously in each situation. Having practical wisdom helps us achieve eudaimonia.

 _____ / 5

Aristotelian virtue ethics does not provide a list of rules for action. Instead, knowing what is the morally correct action requires the intellectual virtue of practical wisdom (phronesis). Practical wisdom requires a general understanding of eudaimonia (human flourishing) and then the ability to apply this understanding to the specific details of a situation – the time, the place, the people involved, etc. Practical wisdom then involves deliberation (thinking through the possible courses of action) and then judging what needs to be done to achieve a virtuous outcome. Finally, practical wisdom involves acting in a virtuous way to successfully achieve this virtuous outcome.

 _____ / 5

## Assess Aristotelian virtue ethics.    *(25 marks)*

Use the spaces below to plan a consistent and balanced response to this 25 mark question on virtue ethics.

Introduction: In this essay I will argue that _____
_____ .

Argument for my side: _____

_____ .

Response to this argument: _____

_____ .

Counter-response defending my side: _____

_____ .

Objection to my side: _____

_____ .

Response to this objection defending my side: _____

_____ .

Extra space: _____

_____

_____

_____ .

**Exam tip:**

There are only so many potential essay topics, so plan what you're going to argue for each one **before** the exam.

Conclusion: _____

_____ .

# Metaethics

**(?) Multiple choice: Select the correct answer(s) from the boxes below.**

What do **moral anti-realists** believe?

☐ Moral judgements express facts.

☐ Moral judgements are non-cognitive.

☐ Moral properties and facts do not exist.

☐ Moral judgements describe the world.

---

**→ Match the metaethical theory (left) to its description (right).**

1. Naturalism        A. Moral statements are non-cognitive and express instructions

2. Non-naturalism    B. Moral statements are cognitive, moral properties are natural

3. Error theory      C. Moral statements are non-cognitive and express feelings

4. Emotivism         D. Moral statements are cognitive, moral properties aren't natural

5. Prescriptivism    E. Moral statements are cognitive, moral properties don't exist

---

**(?) Cognitive or non-cognitive statement? Cross out the wrong answer for each.**

| Today is Friday. | Cognitive / Non-cognitive |
|---|---|
| Hooray! Friday! | Cognitive / Non-cognitive |
| I like Fridays. | Cognitive / Non-cognitive |
| Have a nice weekend! | Cognitive / Non-cognitive |

---

**(?) Multiple choice: Select the correct answer(s) from the boxes below.**

**Utilitarianism** is an example of which metaethical theory?

☐ Moral naturalism.

☐ Error theory.

☐ Emotivism.

☐ Prescriptivism.

## What is moral realism?        (3 marks)

Moral realism is the view that mind-independent moral _____ and

_____ do exist. For example, 'good', '_____', 'right',

and '_____' exist objectively and mind-independently.


## What does it mean to be a non-cognitivist about moral language?        (3 marks)

**Cross out the wrong answers below, leaving the correct descriptions.**

Moral non-cognitivism is the view that moral judgements _do / do not_ aim to describe

the (mind-independent) world and so _are / are not_ capable of being true or false. For

example _prescriptivism / naturalism_ is non-cognitivist because it says moral

judgments express _instructions / beliefs_ (e.g. "don't do that!").


## Outline Mackie's error theory.        (5 marks)

Error theory says moral judgements are _____ and so should be

understood as beliefs or descriptions about the world that are capable of being true

or false. However, error theory is also _____ and so says that

mind-independent moral properties and facts do not exist. Together, these two claims

of error theory mean that all moral judgements are _____ . For

example, "murder is wrong" is _____ because the property of

'wrongness' does not exist.

**Outline emotivism and explain how Hume's argument that moral judgements motivate action supports this view.** *(12 marks)*

🧩 <u>Missing words:</u> properties, emotions, believe, non-cognitivist, anti-realist, beliefs, facts

Emotivism is the _____ meta-ethical view that moral judgements, such as "stealing is wrong" are expressions of a person's _____ or attitudes rather than cognitive _____ that are capable of being true or false. For example, an emotivist would say the statement "stealing is wrong" means something like "boo! Stealing!" and so is neither true nor false. Emotivism is an _____ theory, which means emotivists believe that mind-independent moral _____ and _____ do not exist.

According to Hume's theory of motivation, _____ and desires motivate action. For example, my desire for ice cream motivates me to seek out and eat ice cream. However, _____ and reason do not motivate action. For example, if I _____ that "there is ice cream in that bowl" or "ice cream is sweet and cold", these _____ do not, by themselves, motivate me to act in any particular way.

Hume argues that moral judgements, such as "stealing is wrong", *do* motivate action. For example, the moral judgement "stealing is wrong" motivates me not to steal from others. Applying Hume's theory of motivation to moral judgements, the fact that moral judgements motivate action suggests they are more like _____ than _____ , since _____ would not be enough to motivate action. This suggests emotivism is the correct analysis of moral judgments.

**Outline moral anti-realism and explain how moral progress may present an issue for this view.** *(12 marks)*

🧩 <u>Missing words:</u> **bad, facts, false, values, good, independent, properties, true**

Moral anti-realism is the meta-ethical view that mind-_____ moral

_____ , such as '_____', '_____', 'right',

and 'wrong', do not exist. Moral anti-realists also believe mind-_____

moral _____ , such as "murder is wrong", do not exist either.

Moral progress is the improvement in moral _____ and beliefs over

time. For example, in the time of Plato, it was considered morally acceptable to keep

slaves. However, in today's society, keeping slaves is considered morally wrong. This

change in moral beliefs would be considered moral progress if the modern belief

("keeping slaves is wrong") is _____ and the older belief ("keeping

slaves is not wrong") is _____ .

If moral anti-realism is correct, then there has been no moral progress because there

are no such things as moral _____ . And if there are no such things as

moral _____ , it is not possible for the newer belief to be more

accurate than the older one and so moral progress is impossible. However, moral

realists would argue there has been moral progress. For example, _____

_____

_____ is an example of moral progress.

The argument against moral anti-realism can be presented in the format of modus

tollens: 1. If moral anti-realism is true, then moral progress does not exist. 2. But

moral progress does exist. 3. Therefore, _____

_____ .

**Outline moral naturalism and explain how Moore's naturalistic fallacy challenges this view.**     *(12 marks)*

 <u>Missing words:</u> **natural, reduce, basic, right, cognitivist, reduced, wrong, descriptions, correlated**

Moral naturalism is a _____ meta-ethical theory which means it interprets moral judgements , such as "stealing is wrong", as _____ of the world that are capable of being true or false. Further, moral naturalism is a realist meta-ethical theory and so says that mind-_____ moral properties exist and these moral properties are _____ properties. So, according to moral naturalism, the statement "stealing is wrong" is true if the act of stealing has the _____ property of 'wrongness' and false if it does not possess this property.

Moore argued that any attempt to _____ moral properties, such as 'good', 'bad', 'right' or 'wrong', to _____ properties commits a fallacy (i.e. faulty reasoning) termed the 'naturalistic fallacy'. Moore argues that moral properties are _____ and cannot be _____ to anything simpler, such as _____ properties. Utilitarianism, for example, reduces the moral property of 'goodness' to the _____ property of pleasure. But Moore says even if it were true that the _____ property of pleasure is highly _____ with the moral property of 'goodness', it would be a fallacy to conclude that pleasure and goodness are one and the same property.

Since moral properties are _____ according to Moore, any form of moral naturalism will commit the same naturalistic fallacy of attempting to _____ moral properties to something _____ .

*Possible paragraph starters:*

**Introduction:** Moral realism is the meta-ethical view that... In this essay I will argue that moral realism is false and thus that moral anti-realism is true.

**Mill's proof of utilitarianism (argument for realism #1):** John Stuart Mill provides the following 'proof' of utilitarianism... If Mill's argument here is successful, it proves that moral properties exist as natural properties and thus proves moral realism is correct.

**Response (Moore's naturalistic fallacy):** However, G.E. Moore argues that any attempt to reduce moral properties to natural properties, as Mill does in his proof of utilitarianism, commits a fallacy known as the naturalistic fallacy...

**Moore's intuitionism (argument for realism #2):** Having shown that moral properties cannot be reduced to natural properties, Moore argues that moral properties exist but are basic and non-natural...

**Response (Mackie's arguments from queerness):** However, the kinds of non-natural moral properties proposed by Moore would be metaphysically and epistemically queer. J.L. Mackie argues that...

**Moral progress (argument for realism #3):** The arguments above demonstrate that both the natural and non-natural forms of moral realism fail. However, defenders of moral realism argue that moral anti-realism must be false due to moral progress...

**Response (begging the question):** However, the realist argument based on moral progress commits the fallacy of begging the question, which is where an argument assumes its conclusion in the premises. In this case, the claim that moral progress exists assumes that mind-independent moral properties exist. But this is what the argument is supposed to prove in the first place...

**Exam tip:**
You don't need two completely different essay plans for moral realism and moral anti-realism. The same arguments that show *moral realism is false* can be used to argue that *moral anti-realism is true* and vice versa.

**Conclusion:** In conclusion, moral realism – both the naturalist and non-naturalist versions - fails...

# Applied Ethics

**Explain how utilitarianism might be applied to the issue of whether it is morally acceptable to steal.** *(12 marks)*

Utilitarianism is a _____ ethical theory, meaning whether stealing is considered morally acceptable or not by the theory will depend on whether the consequences of stealing are positive or negative.

Act utilitarianism looks at the consequences *of each specific* _____ when deciding whether it is morally acceptable. So, if an act of stealing led to a net increase in _____ , act utilitarianism would say it is morally acceptable. For example, if a very poor person stole some food from a very rich person to avoid starvation, it is likely the poor person's _____ would outweigh the rich person's _____ , so stealing in this situation would be morally acceptable.

> **Exam tip:**
> If you're stuck for things to say on an applied ethics utilitarianism question, a good place to start is to think through how the **act**, **rule**, and **preference** versions may respond differently.

However, rule utilitarianism looks at consequences in a wider context. In the case of stealing, a rule utilitarian would consider whether stealing *as a general rule* increases _____ or decreases it. It could be that if society allowed stealing in situations where doing so maximised _____ , people would constantly worry about being stolen from, leading to a net increase in _____ overall. If this were so, a rule utilitarian may take a different approach and argue that

_____

_____ .

## What does Kantian deontological ethics say about whether stealing is morally acceptable?   *(12 marks)*

According to Kantian deontological ethics, good _____ is the source of

moral worth, which means to act for the sake of _____ . Kant argues

that our duties are captured by the _____ _____ , the

first formulation of which says to "act only according to that _____

whereby you can at the same time will that it should be a _____ law."

Applied to the issue of stealing, Kant would say that

the maxim "to steal" fails the _____

_____ because it can't be universalised

without leading to contradiction in _____ .

The reason for this is that if *everybody* followed the

maxim "to steal" all the time, then the concept of

private property would no longer make sense, since

everybody would have just as much of a a right to

others' property as the 'owner'. So, in a world where the

**Exam tip:**

For applied Kantian ethics
questions, think through
the following: Does it lead
to a **contradiction in
conception**? Does it lead to
a **contradiction in will**?
Does it violate the
**humanity formula**?

maxim "to steal" is universalised, it is not even possible to steal. If a maxim leads to a

contradiction in _____ like this, Kant says we have a _____

duty never to follow that maxim. As such, Kant would say it is always wrong to steal.

Stealing could also violate the second formulation of the _____

_____ , which says to always treat humans as an _____

and never as a _____ . By stealing, you are ignoring the owner's

autonomy to choose to give you their property or not, which amounts to using them as

a _____ . This also results in a _____ duty not to steal.

**How might Aristotelian virtue ethics be applied to the question of whether it is ever morally acceptable to lie?** *(12 marks)*

Aristotelian virtue ethics is an _____-centred approach to ethics, which means it focuses on the morality of the *person* rather than the morality of specific *actions*. For Aristotle, virtues are character traits a person develops that enable them to act correctly and ultimately achieve _____ (i.e. human flourishing). Applied to the issue of telling lies, Aristotle describes truthfulness as a virtue that lies between boastfulness (a vice of _____ ) and false modesty (a vice of _____ ). Although this is specifically with regards to talking about oneself, this suggests that Aristotle would not consider it morally acceptable to lie. Aristotle further says that "falsehood is in itself bad and reprehensible, while the truth is a fine and praiseworthy thing", which also supports the claim that Aristotle would condemn telling lies.

> **Exam tip:**
> For applied virtue ethics questions, consider what **Aristotle himself says** and then contrast that with what a **modern virtue ethicist would say** by considering the context of the situation and the relevant virtues/vices.

However, virtue ethics more generally may take a different approach. Although honesty would be considered a virtue, virtue ethics considers the time, the place, and _____ involved. For example, if a would-be murderer with a knife asks you "which way did my victim go?", the virtuous person may weigh up the virtue of honesty against other virtues, such as _____ for the potential victim. Because there are no absolute rules with virtue ethics, the virtuous person must develop _____ wisdom (phronesis) to know when the situation is appropriate to lie. In this example, the consequences are likely to be severe enough that virtue ethics would consider lying to be morally acceptable. So, in summary, what Aristotelian virtue ethics would say on the issue of telling lies is _____

_____

_____ .

## Explain what Kantian deontological ethics might say about simulated killing. (12 marks)

**Missing words:** imperfect, means, universal, categorical, humans, duty, will, maxim

Kantian deontological ethics is concerned with our _____ to follow moral laws. According to Kant, moral laws are _____ , which means one could rationally _____ that everybody in the world would follow that rule. This is the essence of Kant's _____ imperative.

**Exam tip:**
For 12 mark applied ethics questions, include a short description of the theory first before explaining how it would be applied.

Engaging in simulated killing (e.g. in a video game or movie) would pass the first test of Kant's _____ imperative as it does not lead to a contradiction in conception when universalised. This is because _____

_____

_____

_____

_____ .

Simulated killing would also pass the humanity formula of the _____ imperative, as although this commands we treat _____ always as ends and never as _____ , the characters in video games are not actual

living _____ . In the case of movies and plays, there is no actual killing

involved and the actors will have given full consent to take part, so they are not being

used as _____ and so this too passes the humanity formula.

However, Kant's comments on animal cruelty may be relevant to simulated killing.

Kant argues that cruel treatment of animals violates a _____ we have

towards ourselves: The _____ to develop feelings of compassion

towards other _____ . Kant might say that in the same way treating

animals cruelly dulls our feelings of compassion to other _____ , so too

does engaging in simulated killing. If so, Kant may argue that simulated killing violates

this _____ _____ duty we have to develop compassion

for other _____ and as such Kantian deontological ethics might say

that simulated killing is morally wrong.

---

→ **Match the metaethical theory (left) to what it would say about the moral judgement "eating animals is wrong" (right).**

| | |
|---|---|
| 1. Naturalism | A. The statement "eating animals is wrong" means "Boo! Eating animals!" and is neither true or false. |
| 2. Non-naturalism | B. The statement "eating animals is wrong" is true if the act of eating animals has the natural property of wrongness. |
| 3. Error theory | C. The statement "eating animals is wrong" means "Don't eat animals!" and is neither true or false. |
| 4. Emotivism | D. The statement "eating animals is wrong" is true if the act of eating animals has the non-natural property of wrongness. |
| 5. Prescriptivism | E. The statement "eating animals is wrong" is false because the property of wrongness does not exist. |

**? Multiple choice: Select the correct answer(s) from the boxes below.**

Why would **Kant** say we should never **tell lies**, even to save someone's life?

☐ Lying leads to a contradiction in conception when universalised.

☐ Lying leads to a contradiction in will when universalised.

☐ If lying was made a universal law, it would decrease overall happiness.

☐ It is not the consequences that make something right or wrong, but duty.

---

**? Multiple choice: Select the correct answer(s) from the boxes below.**

For which reasons might a **utilitarian** say **eating animals** is wrong?

☐ Animals can feel pleasure and pain just as humans can.

☐ Eating animals cultivates the vice of cruelty.

☐ It is speciesist to privilege human happiness over animal happiness.

☐ Eating animals violates an imperfect duty we have towards living beings.

---

**? Multiple choice: Select the correct answer(s) from the boxes below.**

Which of the following might **virtue ethics** say regarding **eating animals**?

☐ Some farming practices cultivate vices, such as cruelty and callousness.

☐ It violates the duty we have towards ourselves to develop morally.

☐ Animals don't share in eudaimonia, so eating animals is morally acceptable.

☐ If the animal's life has more pleasure than pain, eating animals is morally acceptable.

☐ Some farming practices cultivate virtues, such as sympathy and respect.

# Moral Philosophy Crossword Puzzle

# Clues

## Across

[2] The philosopher who created the experience machine thought experiment.

[3] The philosopher who created the arguments from queerness against moral realism.

[6] An imperative that only applies to certain people..

[8] Singer's word for prioritising the pains and pleasures of humans over animals.

[10] The word for how soon pleasure will occur within Bentham's utility calculus.

[14] The type of duty that results when a maxim leads to contradiction in will.

[17] Aristotle's word for the function or characteristic activity of a thing.

[18] Aristotle's word for human flourishing.

[19] Aristotle's word for practical wisdom.

[20] The mid-point between a vice of deficiency and a vice of excess.

[21] An issue with utilitarianism: The _____ of the majority.

## Down

[1] The only thing that is good without qualification, according to Kant.

[4] The view that moral judgements express beliefs that are true or false.

[5] The form of utilitarianism that looks at the consequences of specific actions.

[7] The non-cognitivist meta-ethical view that moral judgements express instructions.

[9] A non-hedonistic form of utilitarianism.

[11] The utilitarian philosopher who distinguishes between higher and lower pleasures.

[12] The philosopher associated with creating act utilitarianism.

[13] If you have too little of a virtue, it is a vice of _____ .

[15] A belief in the existence of mind-independent moral properties.

[16] The type of duty that results when a maxim leads to contradiction in conception.

[22] The form of utilitarianism that looks at the consequences of general rules.

# Moral Philosophy Practice Questions

## 3 mark questions

What is act utilitarianism? (3 marks)

What is rule utilitarianism? (3 marks)

What is preference utilitarianism? (3 marks)

According to Kantian deontological ethics, what is the 'good will'? (3 marks)

What is the humanity formula in Kantian ethics? (3 marks)

What does Aristotle mean by 'eudaimonia'?

What is moral realism? (3 marks)

What is moral anti-realism? (3 marks)

Briefly outline cognitivism with regards to moral language. (3 marks)

What does it mean to be a non cognitivist about moral language? (3 marks)


## 5 mark questions

What is the difference between hedonistic and non-hedonistic forms of utilitarianism? (5 marks)

Outline Mill's qualitative hedonistic utilitarianism (higher and lower pleasures). (5 marks)

Outline Mill's 'proof' of the greatest happiness principle. (5 marks)

Explain the partiality issue for utilitarianism. (5 marks)

Outline Nozick's experience machine thought experiment and explain how this could be used as a criticism of utilitarianism. (5 marks)

Explain why utilitarianism has a problem of the 'tyranny of the majority'. (5 marks)

Outline Kant's first formulation of the categorical imperative. (5 marks)

Outline the difference between a hypothetical imperative and a categorical imperative. (5 marks)

Explain Kant's distinction between acting in accordance with duty and acting out of duty. (5 marks)

Explain how clashing/competing duties is an issue for Kantian ethics. (5 marks)

Explain the objection to Kant's deontological ethics that not all universalisable maxims are moral. (5 marks)

Outline Aristotle's function argument. (5 marks)

Explain Aristotle's account of moral responsibility (voluntary and involuntary actions). (5 marks)

Briefly outline Aristotle's analogy between virtues and skills. (5 marks)

Explain the role of practical wisdom in Aristotelian virtue ethics. (5 marks)

Briefly outline how clashing/competing virtues may present an issue for Aristotelian virtue ethics. (5 marks)

Explain the objection that Aristotle's virtue ethics does not provide clear guidance for how to act. (5 marks)

Compare and contrast moral naturalism with moral non-naturalism. (5 marks)

Compare and contrast emotivism with prescriptivism. (5 marks)

Outline Mackie's error theory. (5 marks)

Explain Moore's open question argument. (5 marks)

Explain why utilitarianism is a naturalist metaethical position. (5 marks)

Explain how Aristotelian virtue ethics could be interpreted as a naturalist metaethical theory. (5 marks)

How might emotivism be applied to the question of whether it is morally acceptable to steal? (5 marks)


## 12 mark questions

Outline Bentham's utility calculus and explain the issue of problems with calculation (including which beings to include). (12 marks)

What might utilitarianism say about telling lies? (12 marks)

Explain how utilitarianism may be applied to the question of whether it is morally acceptable to [steal] / [tell lies]. (12 marks)

How might utilitarianism be applied to the issue of [simulated killing] / [whether eating animals is morally acceptable] ? (12 marks)

Outline what Kant means by the 'good will' and explain the objection that this ignores the value of other motivations. (12 marks)

Outline Philippa Foot's objection to Kant's deontological ethics that morality is a system of hypothetical, not categorical, imperatives. (12 marks)

Explain what Kantian deontological ethics says about whether it is morally acceptable to [lie] / [steal]. (12 marks)

How might Kantian deontological ethics be applied to the issue of whether engaging in simulated killing is morally acceptable? (12 marks)

Outline Aristotle's account of how we develop moral character and explain the issue that his definition of 'virtuous acts' is circular. (12 marks)

What might Aristotelian virtue ethics say about simulated killing? (12 marks)

How might Aristotelian virtue ethics be applied to the question of whether it is morally acceptable to [eat animals] / [tell lies] / [steal] ? (12 marks)

Outline moral naturalism and explain how Moore's naturalistic fallacy challenges this view. (12 marks)

Outline moral anti-realism and explain how Mackie's arguments from queerness support this view. (12 marks)

Outline emotivism and explain how Hume's argument that moral judgements motivate action supports this view. (12 marks)

Explain how some of the ways we use language, such as moral reasoning and disagreement, are an issue for moral non-cognitivism. (12 marks)

Outline moral non-cognitivism and explain how Ayer's verification principle supports this view. (12 marks)

## 25 mark questions

Assess utilitarianism. (25 marks)

Is Kantian deontological ethics correct? (25 marks)

Does Aristotelian virtue ethics provide a convincing account of morality? (25 marks)

Is moral realism or moral anti-realism correct? (25 marks)

# Answers

*Note: Many of the answers below are not the only correct possible answers, but simply suggestions of what could be written in the blank spaces.*

Page 44:

**Which of the following is not a feature of act utilitarianism?**

*Agent-centred*

**Match the type of utilitarianism (left) to its description (right).**

1= B,  2 = C,  3 = A

**Which of the following forms of utilitarianism takes a qualitative approach?**

*Mill's higher and lower pleasures*

**Which philosopher created the felicific calculus (AKA the utility calculus)?**

*Jeremy Bentham*

Page 45:

**What is preference utilitarianism? (3 marks)**

"Preference utilitarianism is a ~~hedonistic~~ / *non hedonistic* ethical theory…"

"…an act is morally right if it maximises satisfaction of people's *preferences* / ~~pleasures~~ ."

"…It is a *consequentialist* / ~~non-consequentialist~~ ethical theory."

**Outline Nozick's experience machine thought experiment and explain how this could be used as a criticism of utilitarianism. (5 marks)**

"…For example, a reason someone may prefer to live in the real world is *they value being in contact with reality even if it is less pleasurable* ." or "…For example, a reason someone may prefer to live in the real world is *they want to actually do things rather than simply experience them* ." etc.

"…This is a problem for (hedonistic) utilitarianism because *hedonistic utilitarianism says pleasure/hedonism is the source of moral value, but these reasons not to plug into the experience machine suggest humans have other moral values besides pleasure/hedonism* ." etc.

Page 47:

**Outline Mill's qualitative hedonistic utilitarianism (higher and lower pleasures). (5 marks)**

"Hedonistic forms of utilitarianism claim that *pleasure* is the source of moral worth…"

"… (i.e. *pleasure* = good)…"

"An example of a 'higher' pleasure would be *intellectual pleasures such as reading* whereas…" or "An example of a 'higher' pleasure would be *pleasures of the mind, such as art and science* whereas…" etc.

"…whereas an example of a 'lower' pleasure would be *pleasures of the body, such as eating and sex* …" etc.

**Outline Mill's 'proof' of the greatest happiness principle. (5 marks)**

# *4*  All other things humans value – for example, virtue – they value because they increase happiness.

# *3*  The desirability of happiness is "all the proof which the case admits of" that happiness is a good.

# *5*  So, not only is happiness a good, it is the only good.

# *1*  The only proof that something is desirable is that people desire it.

# *2*  Each person desires their own happiness, therefore the general happiness is desirable.

Page 48:

**Outline Bentham's utility calculus and explain the issue of problems with calculation (including which beings to include). (12 marks)**

*pleasure, pleasure, quantify, pleasure, quantify, purity, propinquity, fecundity, pleasure, quantify, pleasure, quantify, pleasure, fecundity, pleasure, dogs, pleasure, dogs, pleasure, equally, impractical*

Page 50:

**Why would Kant say we have a perfect duty never to tell lies?**

*Telling lies leads to a contradiction in conception when universalised.*

**Categorical or hypothetical imperative?**

Don't steal. = Categorical

Don't steal if you don't want to break the law. = Hypothetical

You should leave now if you want to get there on time. = Hypothetical

You shouldn't eat animals. = Categorical

If you want people to trust you, don't lie. = Hypothetical

Don't lie. = Categorical

**Which of the following are issues for Kant's deontological ethics?**

*Ignores consequences, Competing duties, Ignores other valuable motivations*

## Page 51:

**Explain Kant's first formulation of the categorical imperative. (5 marks)**

"...act only according to that _maxim_ whereby..."

"...Kant gives two types of contradictions that can result from an action: Contradiction in _conception_ and contradiction in _will..._"

"...A maxim leads to a contradiction in _conception_ if it would be self-contradictory..."

"...resulting in a _perfect_ duty *not* to follow that maxim..."

"...A maxim leads to a contradiction in _will_ if it contradicts something we must *rationally will*..."

"...resulting in an _imperfect_ duty to follow that maxim..."

**Explain the distinction between acting out of duty and acting in accordance with duty. (5 marks)**

"...To act _in accordance with_ / ~~out of~~ duty is to behave in line with this moral law..."

"...whereas to act ~~in accordance with~~ / _out of_ duty is to choose to act in line with the moral law *because* it is..."

"...in order to keep a good reputation acts _in accordance with_ / ~~out of~~ duty..."

"...because doing so would be morally wrong acts ~~in accordance with~~ / _out of_ duty."

## Page 52:

**What is the humanity formula? (3 marks)**

"...It says to never treat humans as _means_ but..."

"...always as _ends_ in themselves..."

"...all human beings have autonomy and rational agency to pursue their _ends_."

**Explain the objection to Kant's deontological ethics that not all universalisable maxims are moral. (5 marks)**

"...actions/maxims that cannot be _universalised_ are morally wrong whereas..."

"...actions/maxims that can be _universalised_ are morally permissible..."

"...examples of maxims that are morally wrong and yet can be _universalised..._"

"...For example, the maxim *"to steal"* cannot be _universalised_ without..."

"...leading to a contradiction in _conception_ because..."

"...if we say the maxim is *"to steal from shops beginning with the letter A"*, this maxim can be _universalised_ without..."

"...leading to a contradiction in _conception_ because it would apply in such a narrow range..."

"...regardless of whether the shop's name begins with the letter A – and yet this maxim can be _universalised..._"

"This shows that _contrary to what Kant says, just because a maxim can be universalised it does not automatically mean it is morally acceptable_" etc.

## Page 53:

**Outline what Kant means by the 'good will' and explain the objection that this ignores the value of other motivations. (12 marks)**

_duty, duty, consequences, qualification, duty, friendship, love, duty, love, duty, love, friendship, love_

## Page 54:

**Outline Philippa Foot's objection to Kant's deontological ethics that morality is a system of hypothetical, not categorical, imperatives. (12 marks)**

_categorical, hypothetical, categorical, hypothetical, irrational, contradictions, irrational, villainy, inconsistency, categorical, categorical, categorical, etiquette, hypothetical, ends, motivation, categorical_

## Page 56:

**Match the Aristotelian term (left) to its English translation (right).**

1= B, 2 = C, 3 = D, 4 = A

**According to Aristotle, what is the unique function of human beings?**

*To use reason.*

**According to Aristotle, which of the following is the final end for human beings?**

*Eudaimonia*

**Fill in the missing spaces in the table below.**

**Vice of deficiency | Virtue | Vice of excess**

Cowardice | *Courage* | Recklessness

*Shy* | Modest | Shameless

Self-denial | Temperance | *Self-indulgence*

## Page 57:

**Outline Aristotle's account of how we develop moral character and explain the issue that his definition of 'virtuous acts' is circular. (12 marks)**

*virtues, temperance, virtues, skill, skill, virtues, habits, character, character, character, character, character, character, character, habits, character, character, role models, character*

## Page 58:

**Briefly outline how clashing/competing virtues may present an issue for Aristotelian virtue ethics. (5 marks)**

"…a judge who is sentencing a thief could choose to act in accordance with the virtue of *justice* and sentence the thief…"

"…or act in accordance with the virtue of *mercy* and let the thief go…"

"…This is an issue for Aristotelian virtue ethics because *it means the theory is impossible to follow in practice since there are situations where the theory demands two contradictory actions*."

**What is eudaimonia? (3 marks)**

"In Aristotelian virtue ethics, eudaimonia translates as *human flourishing*…" or "In Aristotelian virtue ethics, eudaimonia translates as *living and fairing well*…" or "In Aristotelian virtue ethics, eudaimonia translates as *the good life for human beings*…" etc.

"…It is the *final* end for humans…"

## Page 59:

**Explain the objection that Aristotle's virtue ethics does not provide clear guidance for how to act. (5 marks)**

"As an *agent*-centred moral theory…"

"…Instead, the theory requires that we act how a *virtuous* person would act…"

"…However, if one does not know how a *virtuous* person would act, this…"

"…The doctrine of the *mean* describes virtues…"

"…as not too much (a vice of *excess*) or too little (a vice of *deficiency*) but…"

"…In contrast, *action*-centred moral theories, such as…"

"…if faced with a genuine moral dilemma, such as *whether to kill one person to save two people* …" or "…if faced with a genuine moral dilemma, such as *whether to help someone with a painful and incurable illness end their life* …" etc.

**Moral responsibility: Voluntary, involuntary, or non-voluntary action?**
Sailors throwing cargo overboard in a storm to avoid their ship sinking. = Involuntary
A sailor throwing cargo overboard because he's had a bad day and is angry. = Voluntary
A sailor mistakes some cargo for rubbish and mistakenly throws it overboard. = Non-voluntary

## Page 62:

**What do moral anti-realists believe?**

*Moral properties and facts do not exist.*

**Match the metaethical theory (left) to its description (right).**
1= B, 2 = D, 3 = E, 4 = C, 5 = A

**Cognitive or non-cognitive statement?**
Today is Friday. = Cognitive
Hooray! Friday! = Non-cognitive
I like Fridays. = Cognitive
Have a nice weekend! = Non-cognitive

**Utilitarianism is an example of which metaethical theory?**

*Moral naturalism*

**What is moral realism? (3 marks)**

"Moral realism is the view that mind-independent moral <u>properties</u> and <u>facts</u> do exist…"

"…For example, 'good', '<u>bad</u>', 'right', and '<u>wrong</u>' exist objectively and mind-independently."

**What does it mean to be a non-cognitivist about moral language? (3 marks)**

"Moral non-cognitivism is the view that moral judgements ~~do~~ / <u>do not</u> aim to describe…"

"…the (mind-independent) world and so ~~are~~ / <u>are not</u> capable of being true or false…"

"…For example, <u>prescriptivism</u> / ~~naturalism~~ is non-cognitivist because…"

"…it says moral judgements express <u>instructions</u> / ~~beliefs~~ (e.g. "don't do that!")."

**Outline Mackie's error theory. (5 marks)**

"Error theory says moral judgements are <u>cognitive</u> and so should be understood as beliefs or descriptions…"

"…However, error theory is also <u>anti-realist</u> and so says that mind-independent moral properties and facts do not exist…"

"…these two claims or error theory mean that all moral judgements are <u>false</u> …"

"…For example, "murder is wrong" is <u>false</u> because the property of 'wrongness' does not exist."

**Outline emotivism and explain how Hume's argument that moral judgements motivate action supports this view. (12 marks)**

<u>non-cognitive</u>, <u>emotions</u>, <u>beliefs</u>, <u>anti-realist</u>, <u>properties</u>, <u>facts</u>, <u>emotions</u>, <u>beliefs</u>, <u>believe</u>, <u>beliefs</u>, <u>emotions</u>, <u>beliefs</u>, <u>beliefs</u>

**Outline moral anti-realism and explain how moral progress may present an issue for this view. (12 marks)**

<u>independent</u>, <u>properties</u>, <u>good</u>, <u>bad</u>, <u>independent</u>, <u>facts</u>, <u>values</u>, <u>true</u>, <u>false</u>, <u>facts</u>, <u>facts</u>

"…However, moral realists would argue there has been moral progress. For example, <u>the fact that we no longer consider it morally acceptable to keep slaves</u> is an example of moral progress…" etc.

"…3. Therefore, <u>moral anti-realism is not true</u> ."

**Outline moral naturalism and explain how Moore's naturalistic fallacy challenges this view. (12 marks)**

<u>cognitivist</u>, <u>descriptions</u>, <u>independent</u>, <u>natural</u>, <u>natural</u>, <u>reduce</u>, <u>natural</u>, <u>basic</u>, <u>reduced</u>, <u>natural</u>, <u>natural</u>, <u>natural</u>, <u>correlated</u>, <u>basic</u>, <u>reduce</u>, <u>natural</u>

**Explain how utilitarianism might be applied to the issue of whether it is morally acceptable to steal. (12 marks)**

"Utilitarianism is a <u>consequentialist</u> ethical theory…"

"…Act utilitarianism looks at the consequences of *each specific* <u>action</u> when deciding…"

"…So, if an act of stealing led to a net increase in <u>pleasure / happiness</u> , act utilitarianism would say it is morally acceptable…"

"…it is likely the poor person's <u>pleasure / happiness</u> would…"

"…outweigh the rich person's <u>displeasure / unhappiness</u> , so stealing in this situation…"

"…whether stealing *as a general rule* increases <u>pleasure / happiness</u> or decreases it…"

"…if society allowed stealing in situations where doing so maximised <u>pleasure / happiness</u> people would constantly worry…"

"…leading to a net increase in <u>displeasure / unhappiness</u> overall…"

"…If this were so a rule utilitarian may take a different approach and argue that <u>stealing is wrong even in situations where doing so would lead to greater happiness."</u> etc.

**What does Kantian deontological ethics say about whether stealing is morally acceptable? (12 marks)**

"According to Kantian deontological ethics, good <u>will</u> is the source of moral worth…"

"…which means to act for the sake of <u>duty</u>…"

"…our duties are captured by the <u>categorical</u> <u>imperative</u>, the first formulation…"

"…says to "act only according to that <u>maxim</u> whereby you can at the same time will that it should be a <u>universal</u> law"…"

"...Kant would say that the maxim "to steal" fails the _categorical imperative_ because..."

"...it can't be universalised without leading to a contradiction in _conception_ ..."

"...If a maxim leads to a contradiction in _conception_ like this, ..."

"...Kant says we have a _perfect_ duty never to follow that maxim..."

"...Stealing could also violate the second formulation of the _categorical imperative_ , which says..."

"...to always treat humans as an _end_ and never as a _means_..."

"...which amounts to using them as a _means_..."

"...This also results in a _perfect_ duty not to steal."

## Page 70:

**How might Aristotelian virtue ethics be applied to the question of whether it is ever morally acceptable to lie? (12 marks)**

"Aristotelian virtue ethics is an _agent_ -centred approach to ethics..."

"...enable them to act correctly and ultimately achieve _eudaimonia_ (i.e. human flourishing)..."

"...truthfulness as a virtue that lies between boastfulness (a vice of _excess_) and false modesty (a vice of _deficiency_) ..."

"...virtue ethics considers the time, the place, and _people_ involved..."

"...may weigh up the virtue of honesty against other virtues, such as _compassion_ for the potential victim..."

"...the virtuous person must develop _practical_ wisdom (phronesis)..."

"...what Aristotelian virtue ethics would say on the issue of telling lies is _that lying is generally a bad thing and should not become habit but there may be some circumstances where a virtuous person would lie, in which case it would be morally acceptable._" etc.

## Page 71:

**Explain what Kantian deontological ethics might say about simulated killing. (12 marks)**

_duty, universal, will, categorical, categorical_

"...This is because _there is no logical contradiction that results from a world in which everybody engaged in simulated killing when they wanted to_ ..." etc.

_categorical, humans, means, humans, means, duty, duty, humans, humans, imperfect, duty, humans_

## Page 72:

**Match the metaethical theory (left) to what it would say about the moral judgement "eating animals is wrong" (right).**
1= B, 2 = D, 3 = E, 4 = A, 5 = C

## Page 73:

**Why would Kant say we should never tell lies, even to save someone's life?**

_Lying leads to a contradiction in conception when universalised,     It is not the consequences that make something right or wrong, but duty._

**For which reasons might a utilitarian say eating animals is wrong?**

_Animals can feel pleasure and pain just as humans can,     It is speciesist to privilege human happiness over animal happiness._

**Which of the following might virtue ethics say regarding eating animals?**

_Some farming practices cultivate vices, such as cruelty and callousness,     Animals don't share in eudaimonia, so eating animals is morally acceptable,     Some farming practices cultivate virtues, such as sympathy and respect._

## Page 74:

**Moral Philosophy crossword puzzle**

| Across | Down |
| --- | --- |
| [2] NOZICK | [1] GOODWILL |
| [3] MACKIE | [4] COGNITIVISM |
| [6] HYPOTHETICAL | [5] ACT |
| [8] SPECIESISM | [7] PRESCRIPTIVISM |
| [10] PROPINQUITY | [9] PREFERENCE |
| [14] IMPERFECT | [11] MILL |
| [17] ERGON | [12] BENTHAM |
| [18] EUDAIMONIA | [13] DEFICIENCY |
| [19] PHRONESIS | [15] REALISM |
| [20] VIRTUE | [16] PERFECT |
| [21] TYRANNY | [22] RULE |

# Also available for A-level philosophy

*How to Get an A in A-Level Philosophy: Revision Notes, Exam Guide, and Essay Plans for the AQA Philosophy Syllabus*

Available from philosophyalevel.com | ISBN: 9798719524658

**Includes:**

- Explanation of syllabus topics for all four modules:
  - Epistemology
  - Moral philosophy
  - Metaphysics of God
  - Metaphysics of mind
- Bullet point summaries at the end of each module
- Exam blueprint for each question type with examples
- Example 25 mark answer plans for every major topic
- 3, 5, 12, and 25 mark practice questions
- Revision exercises including multiple choice quizzes
- Glossary of key terms

*"How to get an A in A-Level Philosophy has been a blessing for the teachers and students in our department. Christian's dedication and service to the subject and its students is commendable; he clearly understands the A-level philosopher's predicament and has excelled in addressing this to help them attain the highest grade. A must for every school and college philosophy department."*

- Dr. Rishi Handa, Head of Religious Studies and Philosophy at St. James Senior Boys' School

*"The clear and to-the-point explanations were excellent in clearing up any doubts and confusions. But what proved especially invaluable for me was the very detailed and fuss-free exam technique section, which got me to the exam feeling prepared and confident."*

- Filippo Rossi, 2021 A-level philosophy student

*"Covers all the key content without the waffle and has essay plans for all the main topics. This book definitely helped me get an A\* in philosophy."*

- Meriam Sharkawi, 2022 A-level philosophy student

Printed in Great Britain
by Amazon